1 MONTH OF FREE READING

at

www.ForgottenBooks.com

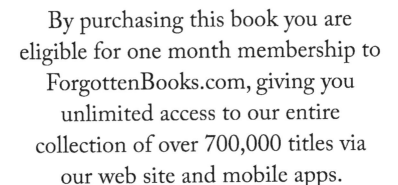

By purchasing this book you are eligible for one month membership to ForgottenBooks.com, giving you unlimited access to our entire collection of over 700,000 titles via our web site and mobile apps.

To claim your free month visit:

www.forgottenbooks.com/free29919

ISBN 978-0-267-62921-3
PIBN 10029919

THE GREAT MUSICIANS

ENGLISH CHURCH COMPOSERS

Printed by
REA & INCHBOULD, 224, Blackfriars Road,
London, S.E.

PROFESSOR W. STERNDALE BENNETT, MUS. DOC.

The Great Musicians

Edited by Francis Hueffer

ENGLISH
CHURCH COMPOSERS

By WM. ALEX. BARRETT

MUS BAC. OXON.; VICAR CHORAL OF ST. PAUL'S CATHEDRAL

New Edition.

LONDON
SAMPSON LOW, MARSTON & COMPANY
LIMITED

TABLE OF CONTENTS.

CHAPTER VI.

CHAPTER VII.

CHAPTER VIII.

CHAPTER IX.

CHAPTER X.

CHAPTER XI.

CHAPTER XII.

CHAPTER XIII.

CHAPTER XIV.

ENGLISH CHURCH COMPOSERS.

CHAPTER I.

INTRODUCTION.

ENGLISH church music began to assume a definite shape and character soon after the Reformation. The encouragement given to the practice of music by the successive sovereigns of the Tudor dynasty, both by their precept and example, laid the foundation of a school of music distinctly national, which would probably have had its due influence over other schools had it been suffered to develop itself without interruption. Beginning with the humblest and most simple forms, the Church Composers from time to time, at no very great intervals, expanded these germs into growths of such unexpected beauty that, though arrested in their full progress, they remain the admiration and wonder of posterity. The English school has the merit, if such it be, of having outlived, in point of relative duration, the majority of the other schools which have been founded,

E. C. C.   B

have flourished, and have decayed. In the long period preceding the Reformation, the names of English musicians occupy positions as honourable as any of those of other countries.

An Englishman, John of Dunstable, who died in 1458, is credited with having been an accomplished contrapuntist, if he was not actually the inventor of the art of *punctum contra punctum.* Probably contemporary with him was Thomas de Walsyngham, Prior of St. Albans, the author of a *Tract on Music,* in which he deprecates the " new character, of late introduced, called a crotchet, which would be of no use would musicians remember that beyond the minim no subdivision ought to be made." A statement in which he was etymologically correct, for there can be nothing smaller than the smallest (minimum).

In the centuries long before, history records the names of Englishmen who had attained some degree of eminence as musicians, such as John of Salisbury, the friend of Thomas à Becket; Adam of Dore Abbey, in Herefordshire, in the time of King John; Gregory of Bridlington, who, in 1217, wrote a treatise, *De Arte Musices;* and Walter Odington, a Benedictine monk, of Evesham, in Worcestershire [c. 1240], a writer on *Mensural Music,* who is credited with the invention of the minim by some writers, but whose claim to that distinction is somewhat doubtful; and others. One of the oldest pieces of music extant[1] with English words attached, has been asserted by Ritson (*Ancient Songs and Ballads*), to belong to the middle of the thirteenth

[1] Harleian MSS., British Museum, No. 978.

century [c. 1250]. It is in six parts, four of which are in canon in the unison, the remaining two forming a "*pes*," that is a foot, or burden. This points to the existence of some degree of scientific contrivance in music known and practised even at that early date.

Nevertheless, it cannot be said that there was anything like a definite School of Music at that period, nor can it be stated with any certainty that the melodies which we call and believe to be ancient, and which have been traditionally preserved, can be positively referred to any very remote age. That music was of general use and in frequent employment, the numberless references in ancient documents, records, charters, and other monuments sufficiently show. The actual character of the music sung or played, even where it is preserved in old writings, can only be guessed at, and not clearly translated. There was no standard system of notation; each writer of a treatise seemed to have recorded his own peculiar views as to the value and power of the characters employed, and the consequence is that nearly all attempts to reduce the music of the Middle Ages into modern notes only result in disappointment.

The knowledge of the fact that Diaphony, Organon, and Descant in their early stages consisted of the combination of thirds, fifths, and octaves, does not alter the position. It should be borne in mind that this sort of harmony was chiefly employed to accompany the plainsong of the church, that there were but few who were skilled enough to preserve an independent pitch in singing the same "tone" a third or a fifth higher, as the case may have been, against the mighty thunder of

B 2

the plain-song sung by priests and people. The solution of the matter is probably this, the plain-song itself was so strongly given out as to render this "organising," or harmony in thirds and fifths, as little offensive to the ear as possible. Written down and sung with one voice to a part, it would appear to the eye and would sound almost unbearable, but given with a body of voices singing the plain-song, it would have no more effect upon the sensibilities than would a light mixture stop in the organ combined with the diapasons.

Such a practice would be perfectly understood and recognised, but it would be rarely written down. It would suggest certain chord combinations which, in the course of time, would be accepted as the foundation of harmony. The knowledge so acquired did lead in time to the formation of certain rules in the treatment of chords which became a system of composition in use to this day, with many of the antiquated precepts still fettering its employment.

The invention of new melodies and the discovery of the possibility of uniting two or more parts in melodies proceeding in different directions led to an expansion of ideas, and taught musicians the need of forming tunes on other patterns than those furnished by the old ecclesiastical modes. The art of imitation, in which one voice suggests a theme to be taken up in turn by other voices singing the like part at the same pitch, or in the octave above or below, expanded into a wonderful variety so soon as it was admitted that there was beauty in it. A greater advance was made when other notes of the scale, or passages of like rhythm, were employed for the answer to the proposed theme. It was thus that counterpoint, at first literally *punctum contra punctum*, point against point, was by degrees made variable in character, even though it was confined within the rules which governed the simpler and more severe methods.

The old composers knew but one process in writing music, and consequently, whether the words they had to deal with were sacred or secular, they had no special method by which to distinguish the one from the other in style of treatment. The progress of the music, its obedient following of narrow rules, was their chiefest care. The art of preparation, percussion, and resolution of discords, the sheet-anchor of more modern expression, being unknown, or if known forbidden, was very sparingly used, and then only by the most daring. Many of these daring innovators were Englishmen. Much of the music written by foreigners in very early times, that is to say, soon after the employment of counterpoint, is not deficient in quaintness, but it would be dry and uninteresting were it not for the charm of antiquity which surrounds it. With English writers the matter is quite different. Although they may have learnt something from abroad, they overstepped their models in beauty of melody, vigour of harmony, and ingenuity of contrivance, so that works by different writers of the same eras, compared one with the other, stand out with distinct advantage on the side of the English composer.

One of the consequences of the commercial communications between England and the Low Countries and the Italian States in the early part of the sixteenth century, exhibited itself in the rapid improvement of church music in England. Before Palestrina—the great reformer of ecclesiastic composition—the Luther of harmony—was born, there were English musicians doing good and honest work according to the traditions of the elders, yet influenced without a doubt by the study of the works of Guglielmo Dufay, Okenheim, Josquin de Pres, Mouton, Adrian Willaert, and others. There is no means of ascertaining whether any of the old English musicians had the advantage of personal communication with either of those great geniuses of their time. The wealthy merchants of England, like Sir Thomas Gresham and Sir Thomas Sutton, men who were so " diligent in business " that they " stood before kings," not only encouraged the practice of music among the people with whom they traded, but also sought to extend a knowledge of its advances among their own countrymen at home, and it is therefore probable that English musicians were not unacquainted with the works of the Flemish musicians who were destined to reform ecclesiastical musical art.

Okenheim, Okeghem, or Ockegem, as he is variously called, may be considered as the point of departure from the old forms of composition to the new. Through his pupil, Josquin de Pres, music became spread throughout the continent of Europe, and important schools of music were formed from several centres.

Starting from Henry Isaac, who settled in Germany, and Johannes Mouton, who established himself in France, and extending later in an indirect manner from Huberto Walraent of Antwerp into England, as it did in a more direct way into Italy, music received its most vigorous impulse through the genius of Palestrina ; and the art attained eminence in each country, developing character in several directions according to the national peculiarities of the people by whom it was cultivated.

It is unreasonable to suppose that the English musicians were insensible to the influence and advantage of these changes. A comparison of the music of the writers of the period, as far as it exists, shows a similarity of thought and treatment which could hardly have had an independent origin. The masses composed by Josquin de Pres for the Chapel of Pope Sixtus the Fourth (1471 to 1484), as well as those of Pierre de la Rue and of Johannes Mouton, were all printed by Ottavio Petruccio da Fossembrone, the reputed inventor of movable musical types, at Venice, between the years 1503 and 1508, and copies of these as well as manuscripts were likely to have been imported into England. In a manuscript music-book preserved in the Pepys collection at Cambridge, which belonged to Prince Henry, afterwards Henry VIII., and in another which belonged to Anna Boleyn, in the British Museum (Bibl. Reg. 10A 16), there are several compositions by Josquin de Pres, by the existence of which it may be inferred that his works were known and studied in our own country. They were probably introduced to the notice of these exalted personages by the "Masters in Musick" who taught them.

The greater number of the compositions of Josquin de Pres and of his contemporaries and disciples were church

music in "Motett" form, that is to say, with counterpoint and contrivance based upon some well-known and
often secular tune of a lively nature.   The word motett
was originally applied to songs whose words were of
such a character as confined their performances to a
limited circle at private times and places.   According
to a passage in the "Roman de la Rose," quoted by
Warton in his *History of English Poetry*, its significance
in the thirteenth century was different to that associated with it later on, and even in the present day.

In the days when the Church permitted the celebration
of the Feast of the Ass, the reign of the Boy Bishop, the
Mysteries, Moralities, and other absurd practices, the
authorities who desired to keep on good terms with the
people would not scruple to introduce at first on these
occasions, and afterwards at more solemn times, their
loose melodies into church undisguised by the graces of
counterpoint and harmony.   It is, therefore, without
surprise that the decrees of the greater powers forbidding
the use of the motett in church are read.   "Videtur
valde honestum esse quod cantus indevoti et inordinati
motetorum et similium non fierunt in ecclesia." [1]   Or
again: "Neque motetos, neque uppaturam [2] vel aliquam
cantum magis ad lasciviam quam devotionem provocantem
aliquis decantare habeat, sub pœnâ gravioris culpæ." [3]

The MSS. of the period preserved in the British
Museum and elsewhere contain numbers of secular
songs by different English writers treated motett fashion,

---

[1] Durandus, *De modo generalis concillii celebrandi*, c. **xix.**
[2] *Uppatura*, a song of a   r fane character.
[3] *Constitut. Carmelit.*, Lib. ciii.

but in which the *canto fermo* is for the most part the invention of the writer. This shows a distinct advance on the part of the English musician; all that seems to have been aimed at by the authors being the retention of the modes of old use, as the bases of their designs and compositions. For this reason there appears to be very little difference to the reader of the present day between the music set to sacred or secular words. The music may be interchanged without any particular violence done to the spirit of the composition. Even so late as the time of Orlando Gibbons, there is scarcely any difference between the style of the Madrigal, which may be taken as the highest form of secular music, and that of the Anthem, the highest form of sacred music.

CHAPTER II.

ENGLISH MUSICIANS BEFORE THE REFORMATION.

THE songs of Robert Fairfax, Doctor in Music of the University of Cambridge and afterwards incorporated at Oxford in the year 1511, who was organist or chanter of the Abbey of St. Albans in the reign of Henry VII., are of the same style as his anthems. The counterpoint is similar in both settings. The only variety which seems to have been aimed at was in the mixture of measures, that is to say, one part moving in duple time and another in triple time simultaneously.

In the volume of music compiled by Dr. Robert

Fairfax, now in the British Museum (Add. MSS. 5465),
there are some songs by William Cornyshe, junior.
These are chiefly remarkable as showing the earliest
use in English music of the first inversion of the chord
of the dominant seventh.

John Sheppard and John Taverner, contemporaries
of Dr. Fairfax, both seemed to have been remarkable
musicians. In one of the anthems by the former
"Esurientes implevit bonis," scored by Dr. Burney, there
is a "regular design, and much ingenuity in the texture
of the parts; three of which having carried on a fugue
for some time, in the fifth above and eighth below the
subject, are joined by two other parts, which form
almost a canon between the superius and second base,
to the end of the movement." [1]

John Shephard, or Sheppard, as his name is spelt in
Magdalen College registers, was educated at St. Paul's
Cathedral under Thomas Mulliner, then master of the
boys. He was appointed instructor of the choristers
at Magdalen College in 1542. If he was in Holy Orders,
as registered as a Fellow as well as organist he must
have been, the date of his birth would be before the year
1520. In 1554 he supplicated the authorities of Oxford
that he might be licensed to proceed to the degree of
Doctor in Music, but his prayer does not seem to have

[1] John Shephard is stated upon the authority of an early
seventeenth century MS. belonging to the Song School of Durham
Cathedral, to be the composer of the anthem "O Lord, the maker
of all things," printed in Boyce's *Collection of Cathedral Music*,
and there assigned to King Henry VIII., and attributed by Dr.
Aldrich, Dean of Christ Church in the reign of Queen Anne, to
William Mundy.

been granted. He was thrice admonished by his own College for offences *contra formam statuti*. One of his misdeeds was entrapping and carrying away a chorister without the king's licence so to do. He probably remembered the custom which was prevalent when he was a child at St. Paul's, and which was still in force at the time of his offence, but was restricted to those who held royal authority for such business. There was a John Shepparde mentioned in the roll of the "Officers of the Chapel" of Edward VI., who may possibly have been the same. His music exhibits distinct efforts after new modulations, and in this respect it will stand well even against that of Orlando di Lasso, in which certain " chromatic modulations," as they are called, are introduced. These are the flattened sevenths of the original key, "premising a passage into the dominant." It is quite possible to believe that Shephard, who was year by year almost the contemporary of di Lasso, did not know of the works of the great Fleming, and that each working in his own way arrived at the same result.

Taverner was organist of Boston in Lincolnshire, and afterwards of Cardinal College, now called Christ Church, in Oxford. His compositions still extant exhibit his great skill in writing counterpoint upon a plain-song or *canto fermo*, as well as in the construction of canons. They also show a decided attempt towards the attainment of greater freedom in part writing, which laid the foundation of the less restricted style which became further developed after the Reformation. His liberal views with regard to the observances of religion entitle him to consideration as one of the pioneers of the great change which was so soon to be effected.

"He, together with John Frith, and sundry other persons, who left Cambridge with a view to preferment in this, which was Wolsey's new-founded college, held frequent conversations upon the abuses of religion which at that time had crept into the Church; in short, they were Lutherans. And, this being discovered, they were accused of heresy, and imprisoned in a deep cave under the College, used for the purpose of keeping salt fish, the stench whereof occasioned the death of some of them. John Fryer, one of these unfortunate persons, was committed prisoner to the Master of the Savoy, where, as Wood says,[1] 'he did much solace himself with playing on the lute, having good skill in music, for which reason a friend of his would needs commend him to the Master; but the Master answered, Take heed, for he that playeth is a devil, because he is departed from the Catholic faith.'"

He was, however, set at liberty, became a physician, and died a natural death in London. Frith had not so good a fortune; he was convicted of heresy, and burnt in Smithfield, together with one Andrew Hewet, in 1533.

Taverner had not gone such lengths as Frith, Clarke, and some others of the fraternity; the suspicions against him were founded merely on his having hid some heretical books of the latter under the boards of the school where he taught, for which reason, and because of his eminence in his faculty, the Cardinal excused him, saying he was but a musician, and so he escaped.[2]

[1] *Athenæ Oxoniensis.*
[2] Hawkins, *History of Music*, Book viii. c. lxxv.

Taverner was not the only musician whose adherence to the Reformed faith nearly cost him his life, but who escaped punishment because of his skill in music. John Marbeck, whose name stands prominent among the worthies of his time, enjoyed a like immunity. Before speaking further of him, it will be necessary to say something more of the musicians who preceded the Reformation. Conspicuous among the crowd of lesser lights, John Redford stands, like Saul, "higher than any of the people, from his shoulders and upward." His anthems and services were many, and the former are among the first set to English words. "Rejoice in the Lord" by him is still occasionally sung in cathedrals to this day. He was Almoner and Master of the Children of St. Paul's Cathedral in the early part of the reign of King Henry VIII., in succession to Thomas Mulliner, and being of a kindly disposition, used the powers he possessed so as to awaken feelings of admiration among his scholars and colleagues.

The practice of impressing choristers for the service of the Church at St. Paul's, St. George's, Windsor, and the Chapel Royal, instituted as early as the reign of Richard II., still existed, and "sondry men with placards," or warrants, had power to take and seize all children "with good brestes" or voices, wherever they were to be found, for the purpose of recruiting the choirs of the above-named places. Thomas Tusser, the author of *Five Hundred Pointes of Husbandrie*, was taken from Wallingford, at that time a collegiate establishment, and sent to London. In a metrical story of his life, written by himself, he describes the circumstances of his removal.

Robert Johnson, Robert Parsons, John Thorne of York, John Charde, Richard Ede, Henry Parker, John Norman, Edmund Sheffield, William Newark, Richard Davy, Edmund Targes, Edward Dygon, Gilbert Banister, Sir Thomas Phillips or Phelyppes, and Richard Edwards, were all composers for the Church in pre-Reformation times, and all contemporaries. There are many of their compositions still extant, but the majority present no marked points to distinguish them as extraordinary.

Robert White, who was Master of the Music at Christ Church, Oxford, at this time, appears by some of his compositions in Barnard's and Tomkin's collections and other MSS. still preserved in the library of the College, to have been a musician of merit. The words of some of his anthems are given in *Clifford's Anthem Book*, 1663, showing their use up to that time. Dr. Burney once possessed a small MS. copy of *"Mr. Robert White, his Bitts of three Parte Songes in partition; with Ditties 11, withoute Ditties 16."* "These are short fugues or intonations in most of the eight ecclesiastical modes, in which the harmony is extremely pure, and the answer to each subject of fugue brought in with great science and regularity."

Sir Thomas Phillips, so called after the fashion of the time because he was in Holy Orders but had not taken a degree,[1] is supposed to be a relative of Peter Phillips, who at the end of the sixteenth century

[1] " Such priests as have the addition of *Sir* before their Christian names, were men not graduated in the University, being in *orders*, but not in *degrees;* whilst others entitled *Masters*, had commenced in the Arts."—Fuller's *Church History*, Book vi. p. 152.

composed the earliest regular fugue known. Some of his writings are preserved in Queen Elizabeth's *Virginal Book*. He was organist of the Collegiate Church at Soignes, and was afterwards in the service of the Archduke Albert of Austria.

Richard Edwards was a man of varied accomplishments, and of a genial disposition. He was born in Somersetshire in 1523, and was educated at Corpus Christi College in Oxford, and in the twenty-fourth year of his age was appointed a Senior Student of Cardinal College, now Christ Church, then newly founded. In the British Museum there is a book of Sonnets addressed to the ladies of the Court of Queen Mary and of Queen Elizabeth, written by him when he was a member of Lincoln's Inn. In the year 1561, he obtained his patent as a Gentleman of the Chapel Royal, and in course of time became Master of the Children there. He was the author of a number of compositions for the use of the Church, and of many madrigals, one, "In going to my naked bed,"[1] being still extensively popular. The fame he obtained in his own time rests chiefly upon his other accomplishments. He was an able musician, an elegant sonnetteer, a ready rhymer, and an amusing mimic. His love for the histrionic art induced him to make the drama a part of the education of the choristers under his care, and with the permission of Queen Elizabeth he formed them into a regular company of players, in imitation of the one which had been established by the children of St. Paul's Cathedral, who

[1] His claim to the authorship of this has been disputed without any very great show of reason.

were at that time famous for their stage performances. Shakespeare alludes to these "little eyesses" in *Hamlet*, and Ben Jonson wrote the epitaph of one Salathiel Pavey, one of the boys of the Chapel Royal noted for his representations of old men. It is possible also that Shakespeare meant his *Pyramus and Thisbe* in the *Midsummer Night's Dream* to be a burlesque of one of Edwards's dramas, printed in 1570, entitled, "The tragicall comedie of *Damon and Pithias*, newly imprinted as the same was playde befor the queenes maiestie by the children of her grace's chapple. Made by Master Edward, being then master of the children." The reputation of "Master Edward" as a poet is well sustained in his *Paradise of Daintie Devises*. His fame as a musician is sufficiently upheld even by the one piece of his work still regarded with favour. He died in 1566 in the prime of life.

Others there were whose works seem to claim a higher place, but whose efforts show less desire of advancing beyond the old established rules. Among these may be mentioned Christopher Tye; John Baldwin of Windsor, to whose careful hand is owing the evidence of some undoubted compositions of King Henry VIII.; Robert Testwood, and John Marbeck of the same town.

Christopher Tye was teacher of music to Prince Edward, and probably to the other children of Henry VIII. He was admitted to the degree of Doctor in Music at the University of Cambridge in 1545, while, as is supposed, he was organist of Ely Cathedral, and three years later he was incorporated at Oxford. His music for the Church was written to Latin words, and it is not at all unlikely that the many anthems of his composition which are to be found to English words in the choir-books of many cathedrals, are but adaptations. These anthems are chiefly in the key of C, and display a considerable variety of invention and ingenuity in contrivance, so that it is not difficult to account for the high reputation he enjoyed while living. He commenced a translation of "the Acts of the Apostles" into English verse of alternate rhymes, but only completed fourteen chapters. He set them to music, much of which, when an allowance is made for an occasional inapplicability to the sense, may be regarded as extraordinary for the time, and certainly superior to anything done by any of the Continental musicians then living. These pieces were sung in King Edward's Chapel, and in other places where choral service was performed, but the success of them did not answer the expectation of their author. It is possible that even in those remote days there was a capacity for distinguishing between the fitness and unfitness of things. His anthem, " I will exalt Thee," which is printed in the second volume of Boyce's *Collection*, is a fine piece of writing, and is considered by many to be his most successful essay in Church music. It is unfortunately very rarely performed now, in consequence of the spirit which exists of thinking nothing good which is old, but which offers encouragement to everything newly issued from the press, be it good, bad, or indifferent. The one or two anthems of Tye's which keep a place in the Cathedral repertory owe their preservation to their brevity.

It is said by Anthony Wood, that Dr. Tye restored Church music after it had been almost ruined by the dissolution of abbeys.

This must be taken figuratively, for it is to others the credit is due, if their existing works be admitted as proof. The same authority states that "Dr. Tye was a peevish and humorsome man, especially in his later days, and sometimes playing on the organ in the Chapel of Qu: Eliz: which contained much music but little to delight the ear. She would send the Verger to tell him that he played out of tune, whereupon he sent word that her ears were out of tune,"— a reply which could only have been tolerated by the Queen without resentment out of consideration for him as her former music-master.

Robert Testwood, a singing-man at Windsor, was held in great estimation for his skill in music, and was one to whom Morley in *A Plaine and Easie Introduction to Practicall Musick*, 1597, accords a place in his catalogue of eminent English musicians. He is best known to posterity through his connection with John Marbeck.

Testwood, who was a priest, had displayed more zeal than discretion in the exhibition of his opinions concerning the Popish superstitions. He preached against pilgrimages, had stricken the nose off a statue of the Virgin Mary which stood behind the high altar at St. George's Chapel, and while on duty there, had sung out lustily during the service, as a response to the hymn to the Virgin, *O redemptrix et salvatrix*, "Non redemptrix nec salvatrix." For these and for like offences he was tried, condemned, and burnt, with two others named Person and Filmer. John Marbeck was included in the same indictment, but "being a man of meek and harmless temper, and highly esteemed for his skill in music, was remitted to Gardiner, who was both his patron and persecutor, in order either to his purgation, or a discovery of others who might have contracted the taint of heresy; but under the greatest of all temptations he behaved with the utmost integrity and uprightness, and refusing to make any discoveries to the hurt of others, he, through the intercession of Sir Humfrey Foster, obtained the king's pardon." He employed the liberty he gained in completing a Concordance of the Scriptures he had commenced, and published in 1550 *The Boke of Common Praier, noted.*

Collier, in his *Ecclesiastical History*, says that Archbishop Cranmer was the first who arranged the translation of the Litany to a chant. This was partly in fulfilment of a command of the king for a translation of certain Processions to be used upon festival days, for in a letter written by the Prelate to His Highness in 1545, he says: "After your Highness has corrected it, if your Grace commands some devout and solemn note to be made thereunto, I trust it will much excitate and stir the hearts of all men to devotion and godliness. But in my opinion, the song that shall be made thereunto would not be full of notes, but, as near as may be, for every syllable a note, so that it may be sung distinctly and devoutly. As concerning the *Salva festa dies*, the Latin note, as I think, is sober and distinct enough. Wherefore I have travailed to make the verses in *English*, and have put the Latin note into the same. Nevertheless, those that be cunning in singing can make a much more solemn note thereto. I made them only for a proof, to see how English would do in a Song." The Litany so adapted by Cranmer is probably that which is in use to this day. Marbeck did not include the Litany in his Service-book, as he probably sought only to present those portions of the Service to English words for which no former provision was made. The Litany in English was first sung in St. Paul's Cathedral on the 18th September, 1547, the priests and clerks all kneeling, Cranmer's adaptation probably being used. This was the first time any portion of the service was publicly performed in the vulgar tongue, and from this day commences the history of English Church Composers.

CHAPTER III.

THOMAS TALLIS AND RICHARD FARRANT.

THE name of THOMAS TALLIS heads the list of English Church Composers of eminence of this period, as well by reason of priority of age as for the services he rendered to his art. The date of his birth is not exactly known. He is said to have been born early in the reign of Henry VIII. He died in 1585. If he was then seventy years of age, as is supposed, he must have first seen the light in the sixth year of Henry's reign. The particulars of his early education are indefinite. He was a pupil of Thomas Mulliner, and fellow chorister of John Redford, of St. Paul's. It is supposed that as soon as his voice broke he was nominated organist at Waltham Abbey, but nothing certain is known beyond the fact that he held the place in 1540, when the last abbot, Thomas Fuller, surrendered to Henry VIII. He was appointed a Gentleman of the Chapel Royal about the year 1542, and served King Henry VIII., King Edward, Queen Mary, and Queen Elizabeth in that capacity, his statutable stipend being sevenpence a day. On the strength of the title of the " Cautiones sacræ," he is said by some writers to have been organist to the Chapel to the first three of these sovereigns, but this could only have been in his turn. The earliest lay organists appointed were " Dr. Tye, W. Blitheman, Thomas Tallis, and William Byrde," and none received such appointments until the reign of Elizabeth. It was anciently the custom, where an organ existed, for the instrument to be played by some ecclesiastic, or by one of the musical members of the choir in rotation. There are many Cathedrals and Collegiate Churches where organs were known to have existed, and provision has been made in their statutes for payment to organ-makers as well as to those whose duty it appears to have been to blow the organs, when there is no mention of an organist as a distinct officer of the Church.[1]

---

[1] In the statutes of St. Paul's Cathedral, certain poor lads or grooms who were employed, among other duties have their offices thus set forth : " Exculpent ecclesiam, campanas pulsant, exsufflent organa, et omne illud humile officium in ecclesia ad imperium virgiferorum."

Tallis is one of the only musicians of the time who devoted his talents to the production of music of one kind. There are no known pieces by him set to secular words. Unlike the other masters of his own and subsequent periods, he confined his attention solely to the production of music for the Church. The most careful research has failed, as yet, to discover any " songs, ballads, madrigals, or any of the lighter kinds of music framed with a view to private recreation." The character of his music is so solemn, stately, and dignified, that it does not seem possible that he could have bent his thoughts to the consideration of anything less worthy of the exercise of his talents than Church composition.

At all events there are no known secular pieces by him, and his work for the use of the Church remains unimpaired for utility and solemnity; it cannot be said to be of like character with that he would have written to profane words, for there is no means of making such a comparison.

It is said that he was " a diligent collector of musical antiquities, and a careful peruser of the works of other men," and under these circumstances the conviction is forced upon the mind that the productions of the foreign masters were not unfamiliar to him; but that the lessons they furnished were used in such sort as to be augmented with large interest there is not the shadow of a doubt. His famous " Song of Forty Parts," was probably undertaken in emulation of one in thirty-six parts by Johannes Okenheim.

The memory of Tallis is best maintained at the

present time by the harmonies added by him to the plain-song of ancient use in the Church. Marbeck, in his *Boke of Common Praier, noted*, simply gave the plain-song without harmonies, and, although it has been affirmed that he composed or invented these melodies, there is reason to believe that he only adapted the ancient use to the altered Liturgy. Many of his "inflections" are in common employment in the Roman Catholic Church for equivalent parts of their service. Tallis added four parts in harmony to the plain-song, which, for the most part, is given to the tenor voice. In some instances the plain-song is distributed among the other parts, by which it is inferred that he intended his harmonies, with the mixture of plain-song, to be in some sort independent. The people probably knew, and sang, the then well-known melodies to the responses, the priest or chanter first setting the pattern; for the "Responses" in most cases are sung to the same notes as the "Versicles." In the present day, however, when the congregation sings with the choir, they invariably follow the treble counterpoint, and so the old plain-song is lost sight of.

Soon after Tallis is supposed to have completed his setting, John Day, "over Aldersgate, beneath St. Martin's," printed in 1560 a musical service in harmony, with the title, "Certaine notes set forth in foure and three parts, to be sung at the morning, communion, and evening praier, very necessary for the Church of Christe, to be frequented and used: and unto them added divers godly praiers and psalmes in the like forme to the honor and praise of God." In this book the Litany now in general use is inserted. It is different to that of Tallis, which was his own original composition, and never seems to have superseded it in any instance. Among the other works of Tallis may be mentioned the collection of hymns and other compositions for the service of the Church, which he published in conjunction with his pupil, William Birde, in 1575, under the title of " Cantiones quæ ab argumento sacræ vocantur quinque et sex partium, Autoribus Thoma Tallisio et Gulielmo Birdo, Anglis, serenissimæ reginæ majestati à privato sacello generosis et organistis." Each voice-part was printed separately. It is upon the statement here made that Tallis is described by some writers as organist to the four sovereigns; he was so only to one, Queen Elizabeth. This work was the first printed, and published by Thomas Vautrollier, under a special patent granted by the queen. The terms of the document, and the privileges it conferred, show the high estimation in which the patentees were held.

It would be an easier task to collect the titles of the books printed under this patent, than to give a list of the compositions of Tallis for the Church. Many that were known to have existed probably were destroyed in the general destruction of "popish books" at the period of the Puritan domination. St. Paul's Cathedral was at one time well supplied with copies of his anthems. The Rev. James Clifford, Minor Canon of St. Paul's in the reigns of Charles I. and II., in his book of the words of " The Divine Services and Anthems usually sung in the Cathedrals and Collegiate Choires in the Church of England," 1663, the first collection of the kind ever made, gives a list of ten, of which perfect copies of two only are now in existence, namely, " I call and cry," and " Hear the voice and prayer," and there were several printed in Barnard's collection, 1641, with the music. All these motetts or anthems were originally written to Latin words, and it is not known for certain whether he or some one else adapted them to English words for the altered service. In the shifting times immediately following the Reformation, when the law alternately permitted the use of Latin and English in the worship of the Church, a series of Services and Anthems which could be sung in either tongue was useful and necessary, and both Tallis and his pupil Birde wrote after this manner, without apparently any strain of conscience. It is supposed that Tallis, though outwardly conforming to the changes made from time to time, retained his ancient convictions. It is known that his pupil Birde was suspected, and even named, as a recusant, as will be shown in the record of his life and times hereafter. Tallis retained both his position and influence at Court, and, although particulars of his life are scanty and uncertain, it is stated that he was in attendance on Queen Elizabeth at her Palace at Greenwich when he died, for he was buried in the old parish church there in November, 1585. Strype, who wrote a continuation of Stowe's *Survey of London*, published in 1720, gives the epitaph which he found engraved upon a brass plate in ancient Gothic letters in the chancel. The stone in which it was set having become broken, it was renewed by Dr. Aldrich, Dean of Christ Church, Oxford, about the date just given. The church was soon after pulled down and rebuilt, and all the monuments of the many illustrious dead who were therein buried, were destroyed. The epitaph was as follows :—

Enterred here doth ly a worthy wyght,
   Who for long tyme in musick bore the bell ;
His name to shew was THOMAS TALLIS hyght,
   In honest vertuous lyff he dyd excell.

He served long tyme in Chappel with grete prayse,
   Fower sovereygnes reignes (a thing not often seene),
I mean King HENRY and Prince EDWARD'S dayes,
   Quene MARIE, and ELIZABETH our Quene.

He maryed was, though children he had none,
   And lyv'd in love full three and thirty yeres
With loyal spowse, whos name yclept was JONE
   Who here entomb'd, him company now bears.

As he dyd lyve, so also dyd he dy,
   In myld and quyet sort, O happy man,
To God ful oft for mercy did he cry,
   Wherefore he lyves, let Deth do what he can.

It has been stated that the greater part of Tallis's music was set to Latin words. The harmonies to the Responses, the setting of the Canticles, the Creed and Gloria for the Communion Service, were set solely to English ; all the other of his known compositions have Latin. Some of these have never been adapted otherwise, and those that exist remain as they were originally written. The largest collection, besides those in the "Cautiones," is probably that in the volume preserved in the library of Christ Church, Oxford, containing among the works of other writers, several of his compositions which probably never have been printed.

These are amply sufficient to show the independence of thought which Tallis possessed, and also to establish his claim to be considered as one of the foremost musicians of the period, not only in England but in Europe. Dr. Burney, speaking of him and others, says: "Long before the works and reputation of Palestrina had circulated throughout Europe, we had choral music of our own, which for gravity of style, purity of harmony, ingenuity of design, and clear and masterly contexture, was equal to the best productions of that truly venerable master." The harmonies of Tallis show a considerable amount of daring for his period, and he uses with no bad result progressions which, even now, are not freely allowed to students by the purists in harmony. The chief of these is the ascending seventh; that is to say, the seventh in a chord, which according to rule should resolve descending, he resolves ascending. He also employs in his final cadences occasionally, a minor third on the bass note of the dominant, which, followed in another part by a major third, produces to some minds the effect of a false relation; but that the effect is not unpleasing, the harmonies in the Litany, the melody of which was his own composition, to the words, "We beseech Thee to hear us, good Lord," stand as an immovable monument. It cannot be denied that many of his works display a very earnest attempt to impart particular musical expression consonant with the character of the words; but on the other hand, in certain adaptations of words to his music, the sentiments appear to be fitted with sounds in which ingenuity of device would seem to be of greater importance than poetical agreement, and although the mere effects of his noble tonal harmonies never bring weariness to the ear, the desire in the mind to obtain music of a character consonant with the spirit of the words is not always realised.

RICHARD FARRANT, his contemporary, in the few pieces of his still in use, " Call to remembrance," " Hide not Thou Thy face," and " Unto Thee, O Lord," has fitted his words with corresponding pathetic musical expression, and so makes more keen the regret that only a few of his pieces have come down to us. Farrant was a chorister at St. Paul's under Thomas Mulliner, and was appointed organist and master of the children of St. George's Chapel, Windsor (with an annual allowance of 81*l*. 6*s*. 8*d*. for their diet and teaching), occupying, as his predecessor did, a house within the Castle called the Old Commons. He was re-appointed a gentleman of the Chapel Royal on November 5th, 1569, having previously resigned that place to go to Windsor. He died November 30th, 1580, in the sixtieth year of his age. The first two anthems mentioned above were at one time annually sung on Maundy Thursday at Whitehall Chapel, during the distribution of the Royal Bounty. His well-known anthem " Lord, for Thy tender mercies' sake," has been attributed to Hilton, and in the old MS. books of St. Paul's, the Service in G minor, with verses printed in Boyce's *Collection*, is written in A minor, and has " finis quod Mro. Tallis " at the end.

He was succeeded in his place at Windsor by John Mundy, who held the appointment fifteen years, and was followed by Dr. Nathaniel Gyles, in 1595—two musicians of "honest life and conversation," but of **no** particular genius.

Farrant has the honour of being one among the first of English musicians, whose works, still in use in the Church, were written to English words. The anthems mentioned above are not known in any other form than that which they now present. The words of " Lord, for Thy tender mercies' sake," are from Lydley's *Prayers*, the other words from the great Psalter of Henry VIII. If his observance was due to design, he may in this respect be claimed as one of the earliest of the fathers of Church music purely and thoroughly English, even though he did not possess the genius of his fellow-student and colleague in the Chapel Royal, Thomas Tallis.

CHAPTER IV.

WILLIAM BIRDE.

Tallis's scholar, WILLIAM BIRDE, less frequently by deliberate design than by accident perhaps, was very successful in respect of expression. One of his anthems, printed in Boyce's *Collection*, 1760, " Bow Thine ear," is remarkable for the appropriate character of the music associated with the words. This anthem is an adaptation of a Latin motett, " Civitas Sancti Tua," and the sentiment of the words being in each case the same, it **may be** supposed that the attempt to give musical emphasis to the words was seriously made. It may therefore be regarded as of interest from an historical point of view as one of the earliest, if not actually the very earliest, effort in this direction. The like uncertainty which obscures the early life of Tallis also veils that of Birde. The date or place of his birth is not known, but as he was son of Thomas Birde, one of the gentlemen of King Edward's Chapel, and "Clerk of the Cheque," who died in 1561, and as he was a chorister of St. Paul's Cathedral, it has been supposed that he was born in London. The name of William Birde[1] appears in a petition in 1554, quoted in Dugdale's *St. Paul's,* as the senior chorister, asking for the restoration of certain obits and other bequests which had been taken away under the Act for the Suppression of Colleges and Hospitals. He may then have been of any age from ten to sixteen, and thus he might have been born between 1538 and 1544. Anthony Wood states that Birde was one of the children of the Chapel Royal. There is no record of his name on the list, but as the "children" were usually spoken of collectively, the gentlemen only being distinguished by name, the statement is not inconsistent with probability. Until a

---

[1] His name is variously spelt, for in those days there was no fixed rule for the orthography of names, and each man wrote as he fancied the sound should be represented in letters. By this means the writer very often gives a clue to the place of his birth or education not always attainable otherwise. In the greater number of official documents the name is spelt "Birde." Thomas Birde, the father, writes his name thus. In the lifetime of both father and son the name is found as Byrd, Byrde, Birde, and even Byred.

very recent date the master of the children of St. Paul's also held a like situation with regard to other places, and not unfrequently his young charges had to sing when and where the master willed. If, however, then as now, the children of the several choirs formed distinct bodies, unlike the elder members who frequently hold two or more places, it may have been that young Birde was transferred from the Chapel to St. Paul's, for it is certain that his name appears as a member of that choir in 1554. The "Musical Antiquarian Society" printed, in 1841, a mass for five voices by Birde, from a copy belonging to Mr. W. Chappell, said to be unique, which Dr. Rimbault, the editor, asserted was written between the years 1553 and 1558 for St. Paul's Cathedral. If it was ever performed there it would have been about that time, and its existence testifies to the wonderful precocity of the young musician, who may have been at the outside calculation any age under twenty. It is quite within the experience of many choirmasters to find occasionally that the senior chorister is not more than ten years old; if this was the case in this instance, Birde must have been between nine and fourteen when he wrote the mass. Hawkins assumes that Birde was seventy-seven years old when he died, in 1623, this would make the author of the mass, if the date assigned is correct, at least two years younger. The mass is conjectured to have been printed about the year 1580. Birde was then alive, and it may be doubted whether he would have printed a work which he could not but have regarded as a juvenile effort if it had been written nearly thirty years before. There is no title, but the type is the same as that used by Thomas Este, his printer. It may have been published for foreign circulation, or for the benefit of those who carried on the old worship in secret. This supposition is strengthened by the fact that his name was recorded on a list of Popish recusants as "the friend and abettor of those beyond the sea;" this publication may have been the cause of the accusation. As a composition it bears evidence of more maturity of thought than could be expected from a young student, however clever. There is no proof that the mass was ever performed at St. Paul's. It is known that Birde remained faithful to the religion in which he had been educated, all his life; it is therefore likely, if the commercial consideration be omitted, that the mass was written in the hope of contributing something for the service of the Church when the ancient ritual should be restored, as he and others fondly hoped it would be in their own time. The known and certain facts of his life support this supposition.

His first appointment after his voice changed was as organist of Lincoln Cathedral in 1563, his time having been occupied in the meanwhile in a course of study with Thomas Tallis. As it is not unlikely that he would have been quite a young man at the time of his appointment, the date of his birth may be fixed at the year 1544. If he was apprenticed to Tallis, he would have had to serve his seven years fully, as was then the usual custom, from the time of his leaving St. Paul's choir. Assuming that this took place so soon as he was fourteen, he would probably be "out of his time" when he was appointed to Lincoln.[1] Here he remained until 1569, when he resigned to take his place as a Gentleman of the Chapel Royal in the room of Robert Parsons, who was drowned while bathing in the Trent at Newark. His name was enrolled upon the Cheque-book which his father had kept in times past, on February 22nd, 1569. Here once again he was brought into close and intimate association with his master, "That worthy wyght, Thomas Tallis hyght." The esteem with which the master formerly regarded his pupil, and his knowledge of his ability, was probably strengthened by the great progress which he had made in his art during his stay at Lincoln. In the leisure time of his sojourn there he had perfected himself in playing, and if he was able successfully to render such of his own compositions for the virginals as are still extant, he must have attained an amount of skill which many a modern player might envy. These compositions are so contrived as to derive their chiefest effect from rapidity of execution, for the character of the instrument for which they were written did not admit of any great variety of tone or modulations of sound, such as can now be obtained in the commonest and cheapest of the pianofortes made. Many of his

---

[1] This appointment of Birde as organist is further noteworthy. In those days the duties of organist and "informator puerorum" were usually confided to one who had taken holy orders. There is no information that Birde had been ordained, and it may therefore be supposed that he was among the earliest of the lay organists in the Church, or that the Cathedrals and Collegiate Choirs became less exacting in their rules with regard to this matter. In Dr. Bloxam's reprint of the Register of Magdalen College, Oxford, there is a long list of the names of organists there from the year 1483. The earliest of these, if the statement is true, must have been in orders.

secular pieces, such as are preserved in the MS. called "Queen Elizabeth's Virginal Book" in the Fitzwilliam Museum at Cambridge, and "Lady Nevill's Virginal Book" in the possession of the Abergavenny family, were probably written at this period of his life, for youth delights in difficulties which more mature age avoids. There are nearly seventy compositions in Queen Elizabeth's book, Fantasias or Fancies, Pavans, Paspys, Galliards, Almains, and Airs with variations; the last-named are the most curious, the authors being Dr. Bull, Giles Farnabie, William Birde, and others. Most of these have been reprinted in the form most suitable to be sung to words in Mr. William Chappell's *Popular Music in the Olden Times.*

The Music-book of Lady Nevill is in the hand-writing of John Baldwin, singing-man and copyist at St. George's, Windsor, in the reign of Queen Elizabeth. In this the greater part of the pieces are written by Birde for Lady Nevill, who is said to have been his pupil. The titles of the several pieces show an attempt to make programme music long before Berlioz. One is called in Queen Elizabeth's book "The Earle of Oxford's March; the Battell; the March of Footemen; the March of Horsemen; the Trompetts; the Irish Marche; the Bagpipe and Drone; the Flute and Drone; the March to Fight; Tantara; the Battells be joyned; the Retreat; and the Galliarde for the Victorie." The varia-tions made upon these melodies by Birde exhibit con-siderable ingenuity and contrivance, and prove that the players of those days were possessed of no mean degree of skill, if they were able to play the pieces as written, clearly and distinctly. Some of these pieces are in both books, in the one which belonged to Queen Elizabeth, and the other, the property of Lady Nevill; and the only one which bears a date is, "Will you Walk the Wood so Wilde?" This was written in 1590, and is of a less troublesome character to play, by which it may be inferred that Birde altered his views as the years grew on, and was content to expect less from his pupils than as a pupil he might have offered to his master. Only eight of his secular pieces appear to have been printed in his life-time in a publication called *Parthenia*, to which reference will be made subsequently. The first of his works given to the world through the medium of the press, was printed in the *Cantiones*, which was the first book issued under the patent which he enjoyed conjointly with his master, Tallis (see p. 24). This was dedicated to Queen Elizabeth and the preface contained a copy of the patent.

He also published " Psalmes, Sonets, and Songs of Sadnes and Pietie, made into musicke of five parts: whereof, some of them going abroad among diners, in vntrue coppies, and heere truely corrected, and th' other being Songs very rare and newly composed, are heere published for the recreation of all such as delight in Musicke. By William Byrd, one of the Gent. of the Queene's Maiestie's Royall Chappell. Printed at London by Thomas Este, dwelling in Aldersgate Streete, ouer against the signe of the George. 4ᵗᵒ. n.d." A second edition with a slight difference in the title was published in 1588. This was dedicated "to the Right Honorable Syr Christopher Hatton, Knight, Lord

Chancellor of England," and was the first of his works printed in English. It contains on the back of the title "Some reasons briefely set down by th' author, to perswade every one to learne to sing."

1. It is a knowledge easily taught, and quickly learned, where there is a good master and an apt Scoller.

2. The exercise of singing is delightful to Nature and good to preserve the health of Man.

3. It doth strengthen all parts of the breast, and doth open the pipes.

4. It is a singular good remedie for a stutting and stammering in the Speech.

5. It is the best means to procure a perfect pronunciation, and to make a good Orator.

6. It is the only way to know where Nature hath bestowed a good voyce; which gift is so rare as there is not one among a thousand that hath it; and in many that excellent gift is lost, because they want art to express nature.

7. There is not any musicke of instruments whatsoever comparable to that which is made of the voyces of men; where the voyces are good, and the same well sorted and ordered.

8. The better the voyce is, the meeter it is to honour and serve God therewith; and the voyce of man is chiefly to be employed to that ende.

Omnis Spiritus laudet Dominum.
" Since singing is so good a thing,
I wish all men would learn to sing."

In 1589, he dedicated to Sir Henry Carye, Baron Hunsden, his "Songs of sundrie natures, some of gravitie and others of myrth, fit for all companies and voyces; lately made and Composed into musicke of three, four, five, and six parts, and published for the delight of all such as take pleasure in the exercise of that art." Printed by Thomas Este, to whom Birde had assigned the right he now enjoyed as the "overliver" of Tallis according to his patent. The second edition was printed in 1610 by Lucretia Este, the widow of Thomas, as in her turn the "assigne" of William Barley, to whom Este has parted with his right obtained from Birde.

In the same year, 1589, was published the *Liber Primus Sacrarum Cantionum Quinque Vocem*, which was dedicated to Edward Somerset, Earl of Worcester, the father of the author of *A Century of Inventions*.

Birde may have been induced to dedicate this book to the Earl of Worcester out of respect for his abilities as a mathematician. Birde himself is said to have attained no mean proficiency in the science of numbers. The second book, *Liber Secundus*, was published in 1591. In 1607 and 1610, the first and second books of *Gradualia, ac Cantiones Sacræ quinis, quaternis, trinisque vocibus concinnatæ*, were issued. In the dedication of the first to Henry Howard, Earl of Northampton, Birde expresses his gratitude to that nobleman for having been instrumental in procuring an increase of salary to the members of the chapel. The record of this fact is preserved in the "Cheque-book" of the Chapel Royal, with a curse invoked upon whomsoever shall tear out the leaf on which it is inscribed. It was stated at the beginning of the record of the life of Birde that he made the attempt to fit the words he set with appropriate music. This attempt is clearly shown to have been intended in the work published in 1611, with the title of " Psalms, Songs, and Sonnets, some solemne, others joyfull, framed to the life of the words, fit for voyces or viols, of three, four, five, and six parts."

The three Masses in three, four, and five parts, which Dr. Rimbault supposed were written for the service of St. Paul's in the reign of Queen Mary, were printed, without titles, in separate vocal parts, probably by Este, before the year 1590. In addition to what has been already stated concerning them it may be assumed that there were some places in England as well as abroad where the old form of service prevailed, and the need for music was met by the production of these Masses; which are, if anything, in Birde's more natural style. Birde also contributed to several collections by other writers, such as the famous " *Musica Transalpina:* Madrigales translated of foure, five, and six parts, chosen out of divers excellent Authors; with the first and second part of 'La Verginella,' made by Maister Byrd upon two stanz's of Ariosto, and brought to speak English with the rest. Published by N. Yonge in favor of such as take pleasure in music of Voyces, 1588." This was the first collection of madrigals printed in England.

" The first sett of Italian Madrigalls Englished, not to the sense of the originall dittie, but after the affection of the Noate. By Thomas Watson, Gentleman. There are inserted two excellent Madrigalls of Master William Byrd, Composed after the Italian Vaine, at the request of the sayd Thomas Watson." This work was published in 1590. The only instrumental compositions of Birde printed were inserted in "*Parthenia*, or the Maiden-head of the first Musick that was ever printed for the Virginalls: Composed by three famous masters, William Byrd, Dr. John Bull, and Orlando Gibbons, gentlemen of Her Majesties Chappell," 1600, which work was dedicated to Queen Elizabeth. Dr. Burney states erroneously that the book was published in the reign of James I. It contained eight pieces by Birde, and was engraved on copper by William Hole, a process stated by him to be the first attempt of the kind, as it unquestionably was, at all events in England. In the "Teares or Lamentacions of a Sorrowfull Soule, composed with musicall Ayres and Songs both for Voyces and divers Instruments, set forth by Sir William Leighton, Knight," 1614, there are four vocal pieces by Birde, which were the last known to have been published during his life-time.

A vast number of pieces exist in MS. both for the virginals and for voices. The book which belonged to Queen Elizabeth, which is now in the Fitzwilliam Library at Cambridge, contains seventy separate works, mostly Pavans, Galliards, Almains, Giggs, La Voltas, among the dance-tunes, arrangements of ballad-tunes popular at that time, and a few Fancies or Fantasias and Preludes. In Lady Nevill's book there are twenty-six different works of like character. In the Harleian, Matthias, and Tudway MSS. in the British Museum, there are many motetts, madrigals, and anthems for voices, and fancies for instruments; and in Christ Church, Oxford, there are nearly forty of Birde's compositions in a set of books bequeathed to that institution by

Dean Aldrich, who is said to have been the adaptor of English words to many of the *Cantiones Sacræ* which have found their way into the books of various cathedrals in England. Certain of these "anthems" of Birde's are still occasionally sung, and by them is his fame chiefly transmitted to posterity. The canon "Non nobis, Domine," which is generally believed to be his, and which is the best known of all his compositions, is not found in any of his acknowledged works. It was assigned to Birde by Dr. Pepusch in 1730 in his *Treatise on Harmony*, and Dr. Burney asserted that it was to be found in Hilton's "Catch that catch can," with his name attached. This is not the case in the editions of that work printed in 1652 and 1658. The canon is there printed, but no author's name is appended. Dr. Tudway in the MS. collection of music alluded to above, assigns it to Thomas Morley. It is also stated to be the work of Palestrina upon the authority of Carlo Ricciotti, in a concerto published by him at Amsterdam about 1740. The earliest known copy is in Hilton's book, and Burney may have seen an earlier edition than either of those before quoted, an edition which Rimbault says was published in 1651. The subject, which is common property, has been used by Palestrina in a madrigal "When flow'ry meadows deck the year," and Birde employs it himself in "Sed Tu, Domine," the second part of "Tristitia et anxietatis," in the *Cantiones Sacræ*. Handel, Bach, Mozart, Mendelssohn, and others have used the subject, but the treatment is probably Birde's, and could only have been mistaken for the work of Palestrina because the canon, engraved on a golden plate, is preserved in the Vatican, and being without an author's name attached to it, an Italian would naturally be inclined to attribute a work of such excellence to the father of ecclesiastical music in his country. In a poem by Herbert addressed to Dr. Blow and printed in the *Amphion Anglicus*, there is an allusion to this work—

" And there the rich produce doth still remain
Preserv'd intire in the Vatican."

The marginal note to this explains it to mean " Bird's Anthem in Golden notes." The evidence is therefore in favour of the claim made for our early English musician, if the " Canon " is understood to be the " Anthem."

As a man and as a citizen Birde seems to have been an exemplary character. Thomas Tomkins, his pupil, speaks in his " Songs of 3, 4, 5, and 6 parts," 1622, of his " ancient and much reverenced master." Peacham, in his *Compleat Gentleman* published at the same date, says, " for motets and musicke of pietic and devotion, as well for the honour of our nation as for the merit of the man, I preferre above all other our *Phœnix*, Mr. William Byrd, whom in that kind, I know not whether any may equal."

He was law-abiding though he suffered for con- science' sake. There is extant a list of places fre- quented by certain recusants in and about London in the year 1581, in which there is the following " Item, Wyll'm Byred of the Chappele at his house in p'rshe of Harlington, in com Midds." In another place he is said to be " a friend and abettor of those

beyond the sea." He was then supposed to be re-
siding with Mr. Lister, over against St. Dunstan's, or
at the Lord Padgette's house at Draighton. In the
Proceedings in the Archdeaconry of Essex, May 11th,
1605, "William Birde, Gentleman of the King's
Majestie's Chapell, is presented for popish practices."
His last years were spent in London in the parish of
St. Helen's Bishopsgate, over against Crosby Hall, where
he had for neighbour Sir Thomas Gresham, whose garden
adjoined his house. Thomas Morley, "his scoller," also
lived in the same parish, and Wilbye dwelt in Austin
Friars close by. He was married, and the names of
his children appear in the registers of St. Helen's church
which date from 1565. It is pleasant to believe that
Gresham's design of founding a college for the promotion
of the seven liberal sciences may have been fostered
by the neighbourly counsel of Birde, among other of the
cultivated inhabitants of the parish. One of Birde's sons,
Thomas, was also a musician. It appears that he acted as
a substitute, in 1601, for Dr. John Bull, who was abroad
for the benefit of his health, and read "the customary
oration in Musick" at the newly-founded Gresham
College. The Cheque-book of the Chapel Royal states
that the time of the death of Birde, who is called the
"Father of Musick," was the 4th July, 1623. The
title here given may mean that he was "Father of the
Chapel," as the senior member is even now called; and
as such records only usually relate the position occupied
in the place by the named one, it may have no reference
to his reputation in the world of art. As a rule, ecclesiastical bodies know the members of their choirs only

by the offices they hold, and pay little regard to any reputation acquired outside their own walls by their subordinates.

Posterity is willing to believe him to have been " Father in Music," though his compositions are little known or studied in these days. This can scarcely be wondered at, for men, when they have learnt to read fluently and to express their thoughts lucidly, never dwell with particular rapture upon the beauties of the alphabet, or commend the literary graces of the spelling-book. None, however, would be so foolish as to condemn either as of no value, but on the contrary, fully recognise their importance to the extent of their worth. The musical compositions of Tallis, Birde, and their predecessors, stand in the like relation to musical art as the Horn-book and Primer do to literature. The lessons they contain may be read with profit, and need be studied by all those who desire to know how musical science was treated in its infant stages. The restricted rules which fettered the employment of the chord-combinations allowed in their time were often dealt with so ingeniously as to awaken admiration in the minds of those whose predilections are chiefly in favour of modern freedom in the use of musical resources. The old masters used their knowledge conscientiously, and although they did not despise the advantages of commercial protection for their labours, were not insensible to the claims of Art, as known and practised in their days. Some of their works have descended to the present generation, and are held in high estimation. This would scarcely be the case were they written to minister to a passing fancy, or in conformity with an ephemeral taste. The good is good throughout all ages, and so long as men have the power of knowing good from evil, the oldest heritage from Adam, things which at one time may be deemed old-fashioned will again form a nucleus for admiration and imitation.

CHAPTER V.

JOHN BULL, THOMAS MORLEY, THOMAS TOMKINS.

THERE were several lesser musicians whose names are to be found attached to compositions both sacred and secular, which are still extant, or whose names alone are recorded in books or documents of the time of Tallis and Birde, but whose works have not been preserved. Some there were who were called Church Composers, chiefly on the ground of their having contributed an anthem or a service to the list of cathedral music, but whose fame now rests upon their contributions to the literature of music. The name of Dr. JOHN BULL may be included in the list of Church musicians, although very few of his works or the Church are now known. He was famous in his own day, and the name he bore, that by which the Englishman generally is familiarly called, has induced some well-meaning, but easily-satisfied people to assign to him the authorship of the National Anthem, "God save the King," written, as they say, in 1607, when King James and Prince Henry visited the Merchant Taylors' Hall.

The rhythm and the sequence and fashion of the melody belongs to a period at least one hundred years later.

John Bull was born in Somersetshire about the year 1563. He was one of the children of Queen Elizabeth's Chapel, and received his musical education under William Blitheman, one of the first appointed organists to the Queen, who died in 1591, and was buried in the church of St. Nicolas Cole Abbey, London. Bull was appointed organist and master of the children in Hereford Cathedral in 1582, a place he held for nearly three years. In 1585 he was sworn in as Gentleman of the Chapel, taking his turn as organist according to the prevailing custom. In 1586 (July 9th) he was admitted to the degree of Bachelor of Music at Oxford, "having practised in that faculty fourteen years." In 1592 he took the degree of Doctor of Music at Cambridge, and on July 7th, 1592, was admitted *ad eundem gradum* at Oxford. He was appointed the first professor of music in Sir Thomas Gresham's newly-founded college, and it appears by an ordinance made in 1597, that because he was unable to deliver his lectures in Latin, as all the other professors were and are bound to do, he was permitted to read his in English. The Ordinance refers to— "The solemn music lecture twice every week, in manner following, viz. the theoretique part for one half-hour, or thereabouts, and the practique, by concert of voice or instruments, for the rest of the hour, whereof the first lecture should be in the Latin tongue, and the second in English; but because at this time Mr. Dr. Bull, who is recommended to the place by the Queen's most Excellent Majesty, being not able to speak Latin, his lectures are permitted to be altogether in English, so long as he shall continue in the place of music lecturer there." This permission has been extended to all the subsequent professors of music in Gresham College. When Bull went abroad for the benefit of his health in 1601, he obtained permission to have his duties as lecturer taken for a time by Thomas, one of the sons of William Birde. He travelled into France and Germany, and Antony Wood tells a story of him when he visited St. Omers. There lived there a famous musician, to whom Bull, without making himself known, applied "to learn something of his faculty, and to see and admire his works." This musician showed him a song of forty parts, and vauntingly challenged any one to add another part to it. Bull at his own request, was left alone with the score, and added forty more parts to it. At which the "famous musician," after carefully examining it, burst into an ecstasy, and declared that the writer must be either the devil or Dr. John Bull. In like manner Sir Thomas More greeted Erasmus after some extraordinary exhibition of scholarship, "Aut tu es Erasmus, aut Diabolus."

John Bull returned to England by command of Queen Elizabeth, retained his appointments in the Chapel Royal upon the accession of James I., and, as a member of the Merchant Taylors' Company, assisted in entertaining the king and his son upon the occasion of their visit, before referred to. While the king sat at dinner, " Bull being in a citizens gowne, cappe, and hood, played most excellent melodie uppon a small payre of organs, placed there for that purpose onely," as John Stowe relates. He resigned his office at Gresham College in 1607, on his marriage with " Elizabeth Walter, of the Strand, maiden, aged about twenty-four." In 1611, he received a salary of £40 as one of Prince Henry's musicians, and in 1613 went abroad to the Netherlands again, as the Cheque-book of the Chapel Royal states "without license, and entered into the Archduke's service." Dr. Ward, in his lives of the Gresham professors, suggests as the reason for Bull's retirement, "that the science began to sink in the reign of King James from the want of Court patronage, which it seems induced the musicians of that day to dedicate their works to one another." Bull did not seem to have any reason to complain of the indifference of the royal family to his abilities, and it is probably to other causes, now unknown, that his departure from England must be attributed. The further particulars of his life are uncertain. All that is known of him is that he was appointed organist of Notre Dame in Antwerp in 1617, and died there, and was buried in the cathedral in 1628. Antony Wood states that he died in 1630, at Lubeck or Hamburg, which is not true.[1]

---

[1] There is a portrait of Bull painted on panel in the Music School at Oxford, representing him in the gown and hood of a bachelor of music. On the left side of the head are the words AN. ÆTATIS SVÆ 26, 1589 ; and on the right side is an hourglass, upon which is placed a human skull with a tibia bone across the mouth. Round the four sides is the following distich :—

> " The bull by force of skill doth raigne,
> But Bull by skill good will doth gaine."

The author of *Musique aux Pays Bas*, Van der Straeten, just mentions his name, but gives no particulars as to his life or works in Antwerp, by which it may be assumed that the " Bull

The only pieces of Bull which have been printed, are some lessons in *Parthenia*, to which work Birde and Gibbons also contributed; and two anthems, " Deliver me, O God," in Barnard's collection; and " O Lord my God," in Boyce's collection. There are the words of two other anthems given in Clifford's Anthem Book, 1663. Several anthems, canons, and virginal pieces exist in MS., but the need for printing them has passed away. There are some pieces of Bull's printed in Sir William Leighton's " Teares or Lamentacions of a Sorrowfull Soule," 1614, and in the year 1843 a prayer and plain- chant with organ accompaniment was reprinted. The Sacred Harmonic Society possesses a MS. collection of organ music which contains several pieces by Dr. Bull; and these are nearly all the known compositions of the once great musician. Notwithstanding the small amount of music by him now extant, his influence over his contemporaries and successors must be admitted. He shows by precept and example that instrumental music was capable of independent expression. His vocal pieces that are known are full of dignity and solemnity proper to their purpose, and his instrumental pieces for organ, virginals, or viols, his Canons and Fancies, exhibit great freedom and ideality. In the *Parthenia*, the variations made by Birde on " The Carman's Whistle," are of a more set and artificial character than the pieces by Bull or Gibbons. Birde probably originated the style of making brilliant passages, but never seemed to be

by force did no longer raigne," or else that the Flemish author did not consider it worth while to deliver a panegyric upon one who was not his countryman.

so entirely happy in his mode of treatment as either of the two musicians associated with him in the book. Bull was the first, moreover, who attempted to employ modulations, and although some of his essays in this direction are not satisfactory, as for example, in the piece called "Dr. Bull's Jewel," the transition from G to F, or from C to B flat, still they showed a desire to extend research by not strictly adhering to the old modes to which his predecessors confined their essays. In this respect he may be regarded with veneration, as one of the pioneers of the extension of thought in music, which led to greater results in time to follow. Some of the passages in his virginal pieces anticipated in point of difficulty of execution those of John Sebastian Bach, and his imitators or followers, in striving to do what Bull had done, often exceeded their pattern by adding something to knowledge already acquired.

Thomas Morley the "Scoller of William Birde," in his compositions for voices, his Ballets, "Fa las" and Madrigals, rather than in his Anthems, laboured to do for vocal music what was being done elsewhere for instrumental. His melodies are flowing and well ordered, when compared with those of his predecessors, and this quality has been attributed to his knowledge of Italian writers, who even at that early date exhibited their powers in constructing musical tunes. Many of his madrigals contain "quotations" from Italian writers. Whether in consequence, or in spite, of this practice of "conveyance" it is not known, but an edition of his Ballets was printed in 1595 with Italian words, probably for exportation, an edition of which no perfect copy is in existence. Morley's reputation in the present day is chiefly based upon his *Plaine and easie Introduction to Practicall Musicke,* first published in 1597, and considered to be a book of such utility that editions were constantly sold and re-printed as late as the year 1770. It has been said that Morley's knowledge of Italian musical productions probably suggested to him the idea of compiling the *Triumphs of Oriana,* a set of madrigals written in honour of Queen Elizabeth, after the manner in which Padre Giovenali was said to have collected the writings of thirty-seven of the most famous Italian composers, under the title of *Tempio Armonico della beatissima Vergine nostra Signora,* Rome, 1599. This statement was made by Dr. Burney in his *History of Music,* to support the theory which he strove to maintain in that work, that, however good the musicians of other nations might be, they were inferior to the Italians and probably derived all they knew from them. Other writers assume that the idea was suggested by a set of Italian madrigals, called *Il trionfo di Dori,* printed in Antwerp in 1601, the year in which the *Triumphs of Oriana* appeared. It is a matter of little conse-quence whether Morley was or was not indebted to an Italian original for the "happy thought." The *Triumphs of Oriana* are still known and admired, but few except Dr. Burney would recognise it as a work called into existence by Padre Giovenali.

The date of Morley's birth is not known, though some have fixed it in the year 1564. It is supposed that he was educated at St. Paul's Cathedral. He acknowledged himself to have been a scholar of Birde's. He took the degree of Bachelor of Music at Oxford, July 8th, 1588, two years after John Bull. He held the place of deputy chorister at St. Paul's in 1591, and took his turn as organist as usual. He left St. Paul's in 1592, July 24th, upon his admission to the Chapel Royal as epistler. He published his *Canzonets, or little short Songs to three Voyces,* in 1593; *Madrigall, for foure Voyces,* 1594; *The First booke of Ballets to five voyces,* 1595,—the Italian edition already spoken of was printed in the same year; *The first book of Canzonets to Two Voyces with seven fantasies for instruments,* in 1595; *Canzonets, or Little Short Aers to five and sixe voices,* in 1597; *The First Booke of Aires, or Little Short Songes to sing and play to the Lute with Base-Viol,* in 1600, and edited several other works at various times.

The Plaine and easie Introduction to Practicall Musicke. Set downe in forme of a dialogue: Devided into three Partes; the first teacheth with all things necessary for the knowledge of a prickt song. The second teacheth of descante and to sing two parts in one upon a plain song or ground, with other things necessary for a descanter. The third and last part entreateth of composition of three, foure, five or more parts, with many profitable rules to that effect, with new songs of 2, 3, 4, and 5 parts; was published in 1597, and was the first work on Practical music issued in England. It went through many editions, and was even translated into German by Johann Caspar Trost, of Halberstadt, in or about the year 1660.

Morley wrote many pieces for the Church, but none

of them were printed in his lifetime. A service in D
minor, and one in G minor, were included in Barnard's
collection in 1641, and a *Burial Service* by Morley, the
first of the kind written to English words, is in Boyce's
collection, 1770. The time for the exclusive printing
of music-books, stated in the patent granted to Tallis
and Birde by Queen Elizabeth, having expired in 1596,
Morley in 1598 obtained a similar one with extended
powers. Under his licence William Barley, Thomas
Est, *alias* Snodham, Peter Short, John Windet, and
others, printed several books as the " assigne of Thomas
Morley."

Upon October 7th, 1602, George Woodson was sworn
into Morley's place in the Chapel Royal. Both Burney
and Hawkins state that Morley died in 1604 ; he may,
therefore, probably have resigned, as there is no mention
of the vacancy having been caused by death. Morley
was a very good musician, as many of his ballets and
madrigals show. His melodies are superior to any of
those by writers who preceded him, and there is no
doubt that the example he set in disentangling music
from the fetters laid upon it through rigid adherence
to certain rules as to the sequence of chords, necessi-
tated by a too slavish adherence to the " Modes,"
entitle him to be classed among those who did much
towards enfranchising secular music from the uses
hitherto employed in composition. From his time
forward writers did not hesitate designedly to set down
melodies which should convey some sort of expression
when connected with words, a matter which had only
been achieved by accident in times before.

The labours of such writers as were associated with Morley in the production of the *Triumphs of Oriana*, Michael Este, Daniel Norcome, John Mundy, John Benet, John Hilton, George Marson, Richard Carlton, John Holmes, Richard Nicolson, Thomas Tomkins, Michael Cavendish, William Cobbold, John Farmer, John Wilbye, Thomas Hunt, Thomas Weelkes, John Milton (the father of the poet), George Kirbye, Robert Jones, John Lesley, Edward Johnson, and Ellis Gibbons, do not entitle them to be registered in the list of Church composers, although nearly all of them held ecclesiastical appointments, and not a few of them wrote anthems. The titles as well as the substance of some of their productions of this character are still preserved and known.

The charm which is found in the music of all these old writers, and the satisfaction which it always brings to the ear, arises from the manner in which they all employ tonal in preference to dominant harmonies, and further from the tenderness with which the voices are used. " The humane voyce conteines but eleven diatonic notes ; ye doe well and ye use but nine or lesse if so it may be." Wagner, and many of his followers in the present day, have discovered the use of the tonal harmonies ; the value of the limited compass of the " humane voyce " is yet to be revealed to them.

Besides Dr. John Bull and William Birde, the names of John Milton, John Dowland, Alfonso Ferabosco, John Coperario, Thomas Weelkes, and John Wilbye, are named as contributors to Sir William Leighton's *Teares or Lamentations*. The " Songes," as the pieces of music are called, are in the Motett anthem form, in one movement, with points of imitation for the several voices, similar in construction to the madrigals in the *Triumphs of Oriana*. John Coperario was an Englishman who Italianised his name, and who was famous as a writer for the lute and for viols. There were two composers called Alfonso Ferabosco, father and son, who were counted among the most eminent musicians of the reign of Elizabeth, but who do not appear to have held any court or chapel appointments, nor to have written any cathedral music. There is a service in D major by John Ferabosco still to be found in the books of some of our English cathedrals, but it is not of sufficient importance to exalt the name of its author very highly.

One of the first of the scientific musicians who did not think it necessary to keep his knowledge "within the body of the craft," but gave it forth to the world, was Elway Bevin. He is supposed to have been of Welsh origin, but the date of his birth is unknown. Sir John Hawkins tells us that he was admitted to the post of Gentleman Extraordinary of the Chapel on June 5th, 1589, upon the recommendation of Tallis. As Tallis died in 1585, this could not be true. The real date of his appointment was June 3rd, 1605, twenty years after the death of Tallis. He was appointed organist of Bristol in 1589, probably with a favourable testimonial from Tallis who was his master, and here he remained until the year 1637, when he was compelled to resign his post and to relinquish his appointment at the Chapel Royal, in consequence of his adherence to the Romish faith. The authorities were less tolerant to him than they had been to his predecessors. He wrote many services and anthems, some of which have been printed in Barnard's and Boyce's collections ; others remain in manuscript. His chief scholar was William Childe, afterwards organist of St. George's Chapel, Windsor. Bevin's greatest work was that which he dedicated to Bishop Goodman, of Gloucester, to whom he confessed himself "bound for many favours." This was *A briefe and short Introduction to the Art of Musicke, to teach how to make Discant of all proportions that are in use ; very necessary for all such as are desirous to attaine knowledge in the art, and may by practice, if they can sing, soone be able to compose three, four, and five parts, and also to compose all sorts of canons that are usuall, by these directions, of two or three parts in one upon the plain Song.* London, 1631. Before the publication of this book the contrivance of canons was one of those mysteries which the musicians kept to themselves, or only permitted those who were their favoured pupils to acquire a knowledge of. Every canon when given in print was an enigma, the solution of which was known only to the enlightened few. Sometimes, in accordance with the growing fancy of the period and the want of correct taste in matters of pictorial art, the canons were disposed in the form of crosses in circles, in squares, and in wheel-like shapes "very pleasant to behold," but very difficult to sing or play. Bevin's book makes the art of composing canons as plain and simple as it can be. His precepts as to general composition are few and brief, but he gives rules for the construction of canons, and a variety of examples of almost all the possible forms in which they are capable of being put together, even to the extent of sixty parts. His fellow musicians were probably not pleased with him for having exposed one of the secrets and mysteries of their trade. It is a singular thing, that after the appearance of Bevin's book there were very few examples of canons in fancy shapes to be found; his exposure of the art removed the mystery. In those days all men delighted in the occult. Even musicians were not exempt from the fascination of possessing some secrets which they desired to keep from the world. It is supposed that Bevin's colleagues, out of revenge, put in motion the penalties of the law against him, which forbids any Roman Catholic to hold office in the Chapel Royal, and so ultimately secured his dismissal in his old age. If we assume that he was twenty years old when he was appointed to Bristol Cathedral, he must have been nearly seventy when his name was removed. We can at least hope that his colleagues were not so cruel. Nothing more is known of Bevin. After the removal of his name from the cheque-book of the Chapel he disappears from all records. It may be mentioned, that the whole of the examples in his book are constructed upon one figure of plain-song, and the author in speaking of a canon three in one says: "A canon three in one hath resemblance to the Holy Trinity, for as they are three distinct parts comprehended in one: the leading part hath reference to the Father, the following part to the Sonne, the third to the Holy Ghost;" a conceit which Hawkins thinks "devout but superstitious."

John Dowland, Thomas Bateson, and Nicolas Lanière,

are names which are found attached to anthems and to some hymn-tunes of the period from 1562 to 1620, but it is sufficient here to mention their names for the benefit of those who may desire to find them in the list of Church composers. Their worthiest labours belong to other departments of music.

One more name, among lesser musical luminaries, that of Thomas Tomkins, deserves notice. He was born at Gloucester, where his father was chanter of the cathedral. He was admitted as a chorister of Magdalen College, Oxford, in the year 1596, probably between the eighth and eleventh years of his age. He was appointed clerk in 1604, by which time his voice must have changed, and usher in the school in 1606, an office which he held for four years. He took his degree as Bachelor of Music, July 11th, 1607. He was sworn in as gentleman of the Chapel Royal in 1612, and was afterwards organist. He is said to have been a pupil of William Birde. He was the author of *Songs of three, four, five, and sixe parts,* London, 1622; *Musica Deo Sacra et Ecclesiæ Anglicanæ, or music dedicated to the honour and service of God and to the use of Cathedrals and other churches of England, especially of the Chapel Royal of King Charles I.,* and of many scattered services and anthems still to be found in cathedral books. " He was living after the Grand Rebellion broke out, but when he died I cannot justly tell you." [1]

Thomas Tomkins in sacred music, and Thomas Bateson in secular music, were the first who employed what musicians call a discord of double suspension in their

[1] Wood's *Fasti Oxon.*

works, and for this reason his name deserves record, even though his light pales somewhat before the greater fire of Orlando Gibbons, his contemporary.[1]

CHAPTER VI.

ORLANDO GIBBONS.

ORLANDO GIBBONS was born in 1583 at Cambridge, in which place his father held a situation as one of the town waits or musicians. As it is well known that he received his early education as a chorister in one of the college chapels, it may be readily imagined that he had plenty of opportunity of making himself acquainted with the labours of the Church musicians of that time. The new discoveries made in the domain of harmony, the cultivation of melody and canonic contrivance, had all reached a considerable pitch of refinement. Each new composer felt himself bound, not only to know what had been done by his predecessors, but to take up the clue where they had left or were leaving it. When Gibbons began to think for himself the whole of the kingdom was, as it were, surrounded with an atmosphere of genius, which it is pleasant to imagine may have influenced the young Orlando. Like his namesake, he seems to have sought to be chivalric in his art, and to

---

[1] Tomkins also is said to have been the first composer who wrote vocal solos in his anthems; verse anthems are as old as the time of Birde, as Barnard's collection shows.

employ its crudities as then practised, the better to be able to invest them with a certain poetical beauty, in manner like to Orlando in his subjugation of the evil tempters of the desert. The isolated attempts of scattered musicians to add something fresh to existing knowledge were gathered together by him, and employed with greater confidence than heretofore. The music of his predecessors was like the massive grandeur of the Norman architecture—simple, solid, plain and severe, yet noble. The writers nearer to his own date furnished a sort of transition to the style which he introduced, and which may be compared to the graceful beauty of the Early English buildings. The solidity of the Norman was preserved, but the square and formal lines were curved and rounded, new foliage and ornamentation introduced, which, though in some sort still conventional, led the way to the appreciation of decoration in imitated natural forms.

Among his fellow-musicians Gibbons stands out in as clear and defined an outline as does Shakespeare among the many dramatists of Elizabeth's reign. In his imagination, fancy, scientific knowledge, and in his power of concentration, Gibbons may be considered as the musical Shakespeare of his age, though he was not the Shakespeare of music generally. His works were many and of varied character, and possess such an amount of truth in expression that they still retain the power of pleasing and elevating the mind. The actual known facts of his life are few. He was admitted to the place of organist to the Chapel Royal on March 21st, 1604, in the room of Arthur Cock. Here he earned a great reputation as a clever player and "serious musician." He wrote several pieces for "viols in consort," some of which he published in 1610, under the title of *Fantasies in three parts.* This work was "cut in copper, the like not heretofore extant," and was among the first music printed in England from engraved plates. In the year following, in conjunction with Bull and Birde, *Parthenia* was issued. This also is noteworthy as having been "the first musicke printed for the Virginalls." In 1612 his *First set of Madrigals and Motets of 5 parts* was printed, and in 1614 he wrote for George Wither's *Hymns and Songs for the Church*, the Psalm tune, "Angels' song," with several others. In the same year Leighton's *Teares and Lamentations* appeared; for this work Gibbons wrote two pieces. In 1622, May 17th, he received with William Heyther, the degrees of Bachelor and Doctor in Music by accumulation at Oxford, but there is no record of his having been actually admitted to either degree. The eight part anthem, "O Clap your Hands," printed in Boyce's collection, upon which Gibbons is styled "Bachelor in Music," was said to have been his exercise. The anthem is in two parts, the second part commencing, "God is gone up." This division was according to the fashion of the time, which precluded lengthened movements in music. Madrigals were even so divided, and "Fancies or fantasias" were purposely short, and never indulged to the length a modern writer would take to express a fantasia; but then the old writers had something to say when they wrote, and could afford to be epigrammatic. It is Hawkins who states that the anthem mentioned was written for, and accepted as, the exercise of Dr. William Heyther, who founded the chair of music in Oxford in 1627, and took his degrees in 1622 as before said. If this was the case, the University authorities must have been very complaisant in those days. Heyther carried with him to Oxford the deed of endowment of the chair of history founded by Camden, his intimate friend, and it is supposed that the University honoured the bearer with a musical degree in preference to one in arts or laws, as he was Vicar-Choral of Westminster Abbey, a musician by occupation. At this historical establishment Gibbons was appointed organist in 1623 as successor to John Parsons. In his capacity as organist of the Chapel Royal he was commanded to attend King Charles on his road to Dover to meet the Queen Henrietta, whom he was to espouse. Gibbons had to compose the music for this occasion, but while he was at Canterbury he was seized with the small-pox, and died in the forty-fifth year of his age. He was buried in the cathedral there, and a monument was erected to his memory, having the following inscription :—:

"Orlando Gibbons, Cantabrigiæ inter Musas et Musicum nato, sacræ R. Capellæ organistæ, spherorum harmoniæ, digitorum pulsæ, æmulo, cantionem complurium, quæque eum non canunt minus quam canuntur, conditori; Viro integerrimo, et cujus vita cum arte suavissimis moribus concordissime certavit; ad nuptias C.R. cum M.B. Dorobern; acoito, ictuque heu! sanguinis crudo et crudeli fato extincto, choroque cœlesti transcripto, die Pentecostes A.D.R. MDCXXV.; Elizabetha conjux, Septemque ex eo liberorum parens, tanti vix doloris saperstes, mœrentis° mœrentisᵃ."

Of his seven children only one, Christopher, left a name to posterity. He was educated at Exeter Cathedral, under the care of his uncle Edward, one of the Priest-vicars. In 1640 he succeeded Randolph Jewitt as organist of Winchester Cathedral, which place he was compelled to quit in 1644, when he joined the Royalist army. It is supposed that he carried the thousand pounds which his uncle lent to the King, and for thus aiding his Sovereign, his estate was confiscated and he and his three grandchildren were turned out of their home, he being then over eighty years of age. His nephew Christopher was made organist of the Chapel Royal, of Westminster Abbey, and private organist to King Charles II. on the Restoration. Upon the recommendation of the King the University of Oxford conferred on him the degree of Mus. Doc. in 1664. He died Oct. 20, 1676, and was buried in the cloisters of Westminster Abbey.

The printed compositions of Orlando Gibbons, in addition to those already named, comprise Preces, Services, and Anthems printed in Barnard's and Boyce's collections, and in the collection compiled in 1875 by Sir Frederick Ouseley, the present Professor of Music in the University of Oxford. In this last-named book there are thirty-four separate works, including some hymn tunes, organ transpositions of some of the anthems, and the service in F. Some of them are placed a note higher than that in which they were originally written, according to a custom common in Cathedrals when Gibbons' music is sung. In his day the Church tone or pitch was evidently higher than that of the

Chamber tone or pitch, and Sir Frederick Ouseley points out that by raising the pitch of Gibbons's church music, it is brought more into conformity with that of his own time. In support of this statement he adduces the following evidence from the *Pars Organica* of Thomas Tomkins's *Musica Deo Sacra*, a work published in 1668, but probably written many years before, as otherwise the author if living must have been by this time over eighty years old. "Sit tonus" (the note F in the Bass clef) "fistulæ apertæ longitudine duorum pedum et semissis; sive 30 digitorium geometricorum." Now an open pipe of two feet and a half in length will not produce our modern F, but a somewhat sharp G, so it is plain that by transposing the Church music of that period upwards a whole tone, we are, in fact, restoring it to that pitch which was intended by the composer.

The mention of the *Pars Organica* suggests some notice of the organ parts supposed to be played by the performers of the time of Gibbons. In the organ loft at Magdalen College, Oxford, a book of organ music which lay long neglected, on being examined was found to contain some very florid accompaniments to the well known service Gibbons in F. It is supposed that the part was played while the choir sang, and the character of the flourishes was not unlike the extemporaneous descant which country organists were wont to indulge in not many years back, while accompanying the Chants and Psalms. The passages in the organ part referred to bear some similarity to certain parts of the virginal music in *Parthenia*. There is no direct evidence that such was the manner in which organists were wont to accompany vocal music in the service; possibly such an arrangement may represent some effort of a composer, perhaps Benjamin Rogers, to supply a florid part for the organ after the prevailing fashion as regards compositions for the virginals.

The list of printed music of Gibbons as compiled by Mr. Husk, may be seen *sub voce* Gibbons, in *Grove's Dictionary*.

CHAPTER VII.

HENRY LAWES, ADRIAN BATTEN, WILLIAM CHILDE, BENJAMIN ROGERS, MATTHEW LOCK.

IT will be noticed in the list of works by Gibbons, that two of the five-voice verse anthems are with viols. This statement indicates a somewhat early use of those instruments of accompaniment to sacred music; the parts are in unison with the voices, as was then common when they were employed. There was no attempt at independence of treatment, except in certain *ritornelli* passages while the voices were at rest. It has been asserted, and the supposition is a likely one, that "viols" were used to accompany the verse or soli parts, the full or chorus passages being supported by the organ. In the time of Gibbons the viol was coming into use, and as it was a fashionable instrument, the musicians of the period wrote frequently for it. Gibbons composed some *Fancies* for viols, and the celebrated John Jenkins,[1] "the little man

[1] B. 1592, D. 1678.

with a great soul," did much to popularise the music of viols by his compositions for them in "Consort." Gibbons was not equal to Jenkins in his instrumental works, but in vocal music he stands alone, and for his skill, his invention and facility, truly deserves the title by which he has been sometimes called, "The English Palestrina."

In some respects Gibbons was more in advance of his time than Palestrina was in his, inasmuch as without actually foreseeing what might be the outcome of the endeavour to free musical composition from what may be called ecclesiastical restraint, he made one of the first attempts to go farther a-field than the composers of times before had permitted themselves to stray.

Most Church music was written in the Dorian mode, that is to say, in the key of D minor made out of the notes of the scale of C. Other modes were occasionally employed, such as the Hypodorian, the scale of A minor; the Lydian and the Hypolydian, the scale of F with a sharp fourth, and that of C as it stands normally. Thus Tallis's service is said to be in D minor, when, as neither sharp nor flat is placed at the beginning, which in old times only exhibited the shifting of the mode, not the change of key, it is in the Dorian mode.

When sharps and flats became general in use in composition, it was to show modulation. These modulations led to the employment of different scales at different pitches, but it was not until the time of Gibbons, and well on into the reign of Charles the First, that musicians thought of employing any other modes than those which would be represented in modern notation by the **key** signatures of C, F, and occasionally but very rarely G, and their relative minors. The attempts at modulation would doubtless teach one thing, namely, that it was possible to make excursions into "remote keys" in such a manner as to avoid the "wolf," then to be found in all instruments of absolute pitch, whether of pipes, with strings, or with fretted finger-boards. These transitory modulations would in turn suggest the *starting* of compositions in remote keys, and so augment the power of expression, the great charm of music, and the means by which the permutations of the scale may be made more subservient to musical elocution. One of the first of the Church writers who introduced expression as a design, and not by accident, was Henry Lawes. This is found in his songs, in which, moreover, he employed such keys as E flat major and C minor actually, though written with one flat less than the signature needs to be correct. Following his example, men began to frame their music to fit the sense of the words, and poets wrote verses the wit and imagination of which have not even now lost their charms. Lawes probably derived his inspiration from a study of the composers of the Italian school, Monteverde, Jacopo Peri, Carissimi, and the lesser lights. He wrote several songs to Italian words after the Italian vein. Hawkins states that, although he "was a servant of the Church yet he contributed nothing to the increase of its stores;" this may be correct in the present day, as none of his anthems are now heard. But if his anthems were like his songs, his name ought not to be omitted from the list of English Church composers, as by the constant employment of a sort of *recitative parlante,* he led the way to a newer form of juster association of music and words, which forms so striking a feature in the anthems of Pelham Humfrey at a later time.

After Henry Lawes, who died in 1662, there were several lesser writers whose object seemed to be to keep alive the almost extinguished fires of Church music, by raking together the half consumed embers, without attempting to add any new fuel of their own to excite it to brightness and warmth. They preserved the traditions as a body, while only one or two, it may be, ventured occasionally into making some contributions of their own, towards progress. Their efforts therefore are worthy of all respect as representing musical art in Church music, at a time when everything that could be done to crush life out of it was undertaken with a real wanton delight through a pretended desire for purity.

The known particulars of the life of Henry Lawes are few, but a fair notion of his character may be formed from his preface to the first volume of his *Ayres and Dialogues for one, two, and three Voices*, 1653. He mentions having written some airs to Italian and Spanish words. He says that the Italians are great masters of music, but expresses his opinion that his own nation had produced as many able musicians as any in Europe. He censures the partiality of the age for songs sung in a language which the hearers do not understand, and, in ridicule of it, speaks of a song of his own composition, printed at the end of the book, which was nothing more than an index of the initial words of some old Italian songs or madrigals. He says, with some degree of sly humour, that this index, which he had set to a varied air, and when read together was a strange medley of nonsense, passed with a great part of the world as an Italian song.

In the year 1633 Henry Lawes and Simon Ives were ordered to compose the music to a masque, afterwards presented at Whitehall on Candlemas night (Feb. 2,) before the King and Queen, by the gentlemen of the four Inns of Court; for which they received the sum of one hundred pounds. Lawes also set Milton's "Comus," which was represented at Ludlow Castle on Michaelmas night in 1634. Milton's friendship for the musician is supposed to have dated from this time. He inscribed a sonnet to him, commencing "Harry, whose tuneful and well measured song." Other poets of the period laboured to do him honour in verse, but poets are not prophets, and the exalted estimation of posterity for his music, which they one and all foretold, has not been realised. In one respect the musicians of posterity ought to be grateful to Lawes, as he was the first musician who employed bars to his music to mark the place of accent and the rhythmical division of the melody, after the now common practice. What Lawes did in his secular music Adrian Batten seems to haved one in his Church compositions. His anthems, *Deliver us, O Lord*, and *Lord we beseech Thee*, in an old MS. book belonging to St. Paul's Cathedral, have bars at regular intervals. The character of his music is good and devotional, so that Burney was scarcely justified in saying, " he was a good harmonist of the old school, without adding anything to the common stock of ideas in melody or modulation with which the art was furnished long before he was born. Nor did he correct any of the errors in accent with which former times abounded." It is somewhat singular that the two men who were doing like work in different degrees, should be so spoken of by the two historians of music, Hawkins and Burney. Batten was probably born at Winchester about the year 1590. He was a chorister in the cathedral there under John Holmes the organist, and was appointed vicar-choral of Westminster Abbey in 1614, and ten years later removed to St. Paul's to become vicar-choral, and organist. His death is supposed to have taken place soon after the year 1649.

William Childe, Benjamin Rogers and Matthew Lock, were the other musicians of name who were men at the time of the Interregnum between the death of Charles the First and the restoration of his son.

William Childe was born at Bristol in 1605, and became the pupil of Elway Bevin. In 1631 he graduated Bachelor in Music at Oxford, and upon the death of Dr. Nathaniel Giles succeeded him as organist and master of the children in 1633. He was made one of the organists at the Chapel Royal after the Restoration, and took his doctor's degree in 1663. His compositions are of no particular originality. He apparently took Gibbons as his model, and constructed his music in imitation of his greater colleague. His *sharp service* [in D], as a composition in the major was then called, was a great favourite with Charles the First, and contains such an amount of intricate contrivance that his contemporaries, knowing the general fashion of his compositions, doubted whether he was the author of it. It was said to have been written to puzzle the choirmen by its complications, they having laughed at some of his music because it was so easy. He died March 23, 1697, in the ninety-first year of his age. He gave twenty pounds towards building the town-hall at Windsor, and fifty pounds to the corporation to be disposed in charitable uses. His name is associated with an act of liberality which deserves to be recorded. Some time before his death he promised to repair the choir of the chapel, if the Dean and Chapter would pay up the arrears of his salary which had been accumulating for many years. They paid the money, and he performed his promise; " neither they nor the Knights Companions of the most noble Order of the Garter interposing to prevent it, or signifying the least inclination to share with a servant and dependant of theirs iu the honour of so munificent an act." Dr. Childe was appointed to Windsor just as Benjamin Rogers went out into the world. Young Rogers had been the pupil of Dr. Nathaniel Giles, and was about 19 years old when his master died; it is not at all likely that Dr. Childe had any hand in his musical education, though it has been so stated. Benjamin, the son of Peter Rogers, one of the singing-men of St. George's Chapel, Windsor, was born in 1614, and brought up as a chorister there. He was afterwards a singing-man in the same chapel. He was appointed organist of Christ Church, Dublin, but left that place when the rebellion broke out in 1641, and returned to Windsor, where he once more obtained a singing-man's place. He continued to exercise himself in composition, and in 1653 wrote some airs for viols and organ which were sent as great rarities to the court of the Arch-Duke Leopold, and by him greatly admired. The Germans of those days had not attained any such eminence as composers as the English. In 1658 his friend Dr. Nathaniel Ingelo, of Eton College, obtained letters of recommendation from Oliver Cromwell to the University of Cambridge to confer the degree of Bachelor of Music upon him, which was done, he being matriculated as a member of Queen's College. When Dr. Ingelo went to Sweden as chaplain to Lord Whitlock, he took with him several compositions of Rogers's "which were played several times before Queen Christina with great liking." The *Hymnus Eucharisticus*, now sung as part of the grace at the *Gaudy*, on July 22, at Magdalen College, Oxford, was written by Dr. Ingelo, and Rogers set it to music of four parts. It was first performed at a feast at which the Lord Mayor, aldermen, and chief citizens of London entertained the king, the two dukes, and both Houses of Parliament. The hymn was afterwards altered for Magdalen College, and is now annually sung on the top of the tower of the college at five o'clock on May-day morning. About the year 1661 he was appointed organist of Eton College. He was made organist of Magdalen College, Oxford, on July 22, 1664, and entered upon his duties on the 25th of January in the following year. He was to receive the sum of sixty pounds a year, and lodgings in the college, the largest sum ever paid to the organist and *informator choristarum* up to that time. This agreement was not entered into without objections on the part of some of the Fellows, but when it was explained that " it was little enough for a man of that quality, at a time when organists were scarce," we are further told that "nor had any man there to object against it." He held the place until the year 1685, when he was dismissed by the College, and not, as Hawkins says, " ejected by order of James II." The king's edict was not promulgated until the following year. Benjamin Rogers was dismissed for his own misdemeanours, and because of the scandalous behaviour of his daughter. The College gave him a pension of 30*l*. for life. He died, at the age of 84, in 1698, and was buried on the 21st June in that year in the church of St. Peter le Bailey, in which parish he had lived his last years. He took his degree of Doctor of Music July 12, 1669, his music being the first ever performed in the Sheldonian Theatre, " the third day after the opening and dedication of the said theatre to a learned use."

Dr. Rogers wrote much music for the Church ; services in F, as well as in D, A, and E, over twenty anthems, some half dozen pieces to sacred Latin words, four part songs, printed in Playford's " Musical Companion," 1673, and a large number of instrumental pieces. The services are in constant use, but only three of his anthems are generally known, *Behold, now praise the Lord; Teach me, O Lord;* and *Lord, who shall dwell.* The adherence to ancient practices is exemplified in some of his sacred music. The anthem *Teach me, O Lord*, is actually in the key of A, but there are only two sharps to the signature. The indication of a leaning towards the disregard of ancient rules gives one of the peculiarities to his music. When he employs the seventh in a chord he frequently makes it ascend before resolving, a practice which is contrary to precept.

A curious fact is stated by Humphrey Wanley to Samuel Pepys, in a letter dated June 25, 1699, which will be interesting to students of ancient Greek music. " Three tunes of the ancient Greek music are hymns of one Dionysius, inscribed ἐις Μοῦσαν ἐις 'Απολλωνα, and ἐις Νέμεσιν. These tunes were turned into our common notes, as I have reason to think, by Dr. B. Rogers, at the instance of Archbishop Usher. As for Dr. B. he was well known to be an able musician, but I doubt whether he had much studied the Ancient Greek Music." [1]

It is not difficult in many cases to trace the chain of connection or succession in the musicians of one country in any period, one with another, and it is not a troublesome task to show in what respect Matthew Lock's name ought to be mentioned among the list of English Church composers in succession to that of Rogers. They were associated as authors in the publication of some instrumental music under the title of *Courtly Masquing Ayres*. The greater part of Lock's writings were secular songs or instrumental pieces, though it is reasonable to suppose from his style and other evidences that his first essays of composition were in the field of Church music.

As far as can be ascertained, very few of his anthems have been printed, though several remain in MS., among others those that have the accompaniments of " viols, sagbutts, and cornets," as well as organ. His genius found easiest and earliest expression in this form of

[1] Ballards MSS. vol. i. p. 176.

composition. *A Little Consort of Three Parts*, was composed at the request of his old master and friend Mr. Wm. Wake. William Wake was organist of Exeter Cathedral after Edward Gibbons died, and Lock, who was born in the western city in 1619, was educated as a chorister in the cathedral. The publication of this work was made in 1656. Lock was Composer in Ordinary to the King. He was called upon to write the music played when the king went from Whitehall to the Tower, April 22, 1661, the day before his coronation, and received the appointment as a reward. Hawkins says that " he was a man of a querulous disposition, and therefore it was not to be wondered at that he had enemies." He wrote a service for the Chapel Royal, and set the responses to the Commandments ten different ways. This was contrary to the usual custom, and occasioned some opposition on the part of the choir, who seem to have been very childish in their tenacity of newly restored old customs, for Church music had been for a long time silent. Lock was equally injudicious, for he published the service with a preface vindicating his action, couched in no conciliatory terms :—

Modern Church Musick, Pre-accused, Censur'd and Obstructed in its Performance before His Majesty, April 1, 1666. Vindicated by the Author, Matt. Lock, Composer in Ordinary to His Majesty.

If Lock had been living in our own time his trenchant pen would probably have been in great request, and would have found much employment. It would have had the advantage of being guided by a hand expert in its craft. Its lucubrations would have been eagerly looked for week by week. They would probably have had the doubtful gain of securing a circulation for the journal in which they appeared, and of keeping in motion a round of indignant resentment, and so would have fulfilled all conditions.

Lock became a convert to the Romish faith, resigned his appointment in the Chapel Royal, and was attached to the Chapel of the Queen at the Palace of Somerset House, where she had an ecclesiastical establishment. He wrote instrumental music for many of the plays of the period. For Davenant's perversions of *The Tempest*, and *Macbeth*, in which the songs and choruses from Middleton's *Witch* were introduced. Some controversy has been raised as to his right to be called the author of this famous music. Some saying that it was written by Purcell, some by Eccles, some by Leveridge. But Lock's claim has been accepted on all sides. It is amusing to speculate upon the "Observations" he would have made had his ownership to the work been called into question in his lifetime. He was nothing if not controversial. In 1673 he composed most of the music for Shadwell's *Psyche*, which was published in 1675, under the title of *The English Opera*. This was prefaced by a few remarks couched in his usual bitter style. In 1672 he became entangled in a controversy with one Thomas Salmon, who proposed "to cast away all clefs," and to write music for voices after the same scale, indicating the voice by which it was to be sung, by the letters T. M. and B.; for Treble, Mean or Tenor, and Bass. In addition to his compositions, which are of a "robust vein," Lock published in 1673 a book called *Melothesia, or, Certain General Rules for Playing upon a Continued Bass*, which was the first work of the kind issued in England. Some of his Latin hymns were printed in *Cantica Sacra*, 1674, in *Harmonica Sacra*, 1688 and 1714, and his songs in *The Treasury of Musick*, 1669. *Choice Ayres and Dialogues*, in 1676, in *The Theater of Musick*, 1687. Many of his anthems and much of his instrumental music is in MS., some preserved in the Library of the Sacred Harmonic Society.[1] He died in 1677.

Lock helped as much as any one of his time to prepare the way for a more extended appreciation of instrumental music than had existed. Regarded by the light of the knowledge and opportunities composers in those days possessed, Matthew Lock was by no means one of the least important of that group of great musicians which included Michael Wise, Pelham Humfrey, John Blow, and Henry Purcell. Lock lived long enough to have marked the budding of the genius of the latter, though he could not witness its fruition.

Before making particular mention of Michael Wise and his contemporaries, a word or two may be spared to tell of the lives and labours of those who strove to mend the gaps in Church music before "those four bright boys appeared." Among these may be included Edward Lowe, and his praiseworthy attempt to furnish a text-book as a guide to the observance of choral worship, at a time when the Ritual of the Church of England was publicly restored after having been prohibited for nearly twenty years.

[1] Matthew Lock, in *Grove's Dictionary*, vol. ii. p. 157.

CHAPTER VIII.

JOHN BARNARD, EDWARD LOWE, HENRY COOK, JAMES CLIFFORD, HENRY ALDRICH, ROBERT CREYGHTON, THOMAS TUDWAY.

As the events of political history of the seventeenth century are well known, it is scarcely necessary to do more than make allusion to the *hiatus* in Cathedral music during the time of the Commonwealth. A recital of the acts and deeds of the superior powers as directed against Church music generally, and Cathedral worship in particular, would belong properly to the domain of history rather than to that of biography. The spirit of destruction which seized those who obtained the upper hand extended itself throughout the length and breadth of the land. The choirs were silenced, the singers dispersed, the organs broken down, the pipes sold for pots of ale, the books rent in pieces and scattered to the winds, and all that was held to minister to " the beauty of holiness " was destroyed in a frenzy of " zeal," as it was called, but which could only be so if it is the nature of zeal to express itself in wanton mischief and senseless violence. It is owing to this that all Church books anterior to this date, as well as the copies of Barnard's collection of Church music are so extremely scarce. No perfect copy of Barnard is known to exist in any one possession. It was printed in 1641, just before the troubles broke out, and its very newness, and, to a certain extent, its bright and comely appearance—for the printing was very good—may have hastened its ruin. The compiler—the Rev. John Barnard—though no composer, was a practical musician. He held the office of minor canon in St. Paul's Cathedral, and in that capacity had to take part in singing the service, as was the custom for all the minor canons to do until a very recent date. He therefore possessed a practical knowledge which fitted him for the task he had set himself. None of the writers of his own time were included in this collection. Their works were to be reserved for a second series, which, however, never saw the light. It was published in 1641 with the title of *The first Book of Selected Church Musick, consisting of Services and Anthems, such as are now used in the Cathedral and Collegiat Churches of this Kingdome. Never before printed. Whereby such Bookes as were heretofore with much difficulty and Charges transcribed for the use of the Quire, are now to the Saving of much labour and Expence publisht for the general good of all such as shall desire them either for public or private exercise. Collected out of divers approved Authors.* The book was printed in ten separate parts, medius, first and second contratenors, tenor, and bassus, for the Decani and Cantoris sides of the choir. There was apparently no organ part. The several books were so arranged that the side not singing was compelled to count the rests until its own turn came. This may have secured attention on the part of the singers, but it could not insure accuracy of performance. The library of

Hereford Cathedral possesses, at the present time, eight out of the ten parts, and the library of the Sacred Harmonic Society another set of nine parts.

Among the contents are services by Tallis, Birde, O. Gibbons, Mundy, Parsons, Morley, Warde, Dr. Gyles, Woodson, Bevin, and Strogers; and anthems both full and verse, by Batten, Hooper, White, J. Shepheard, Dr. Bull, Weelkes, and Tye, in addition to others by the first seven named composers of services.

With the destruction of the books used in the service came a certain amount of oblivion as to the old forms. When a time of settlement after the turmoil arrived, the older musicians were dead, and many of the younger had adopted fresh pursuits. Few organs existed, and still fewer organists, so that it is possible that very indifferent musicians may have readily found employment, and the more expert were able to command good salaries. Deans and Chapters, and rulers of collegiate establishments, became for a time liberal to others besides their own body, quieting the questioning sort among themselves with the assurance that the large sums paid were "little enough for men of such quality at a time when good organists were scarce."

The Cathedral churches, since the time of the suppression of the monasteries, had been the only seminaries for the instruction of youth in the principles of music; and as not only the revenues appropriated for this purpose were sequestered, but the very institution itself was declared to be superstitious, parents were deprived both of the means and the motives to qualify their children for choral duty, so that boys were wanting to perform those parts of the service which required treble voices. Nay, to such straits were they driven, that for a twelvemonth after the Restoration the clergy were forced to supply the want of boys by cornets (wind instruments of the oboe type), and men who had feigned voices. In consequence thereof, and of that inaptitude which follows the disuse of any faculty, when the Church service was revived there were very few found who could perform it.[1]

At the request of the University of Oxford, Edward Lowe compiled *A Short Direction for the performance of Cathedral Service. Published for the information of such Persons as are Ignorant of it and shall be call'd to officiate in Cathedral or Collegiate Churches where it hath formerly been in use.* Three years later he issued a *Review of his Short Directions*, in which he adapted his original instructions to the newly adopted Prayer-book of 1662, and included several chants and a Burial Service, set by John Parsons. This second edition was reprinted as a separate work by Dr. Rimbault, in 1843, and was included in *Choral Responses*, 1857, by Dr. Jebb. His directions have been for the most part superseded, and none of his Church music is now performed, but these facts do not impair the value of the service he rendered to the cause of cathedral music in his lifetime. He died July 11, 1682, and was buried in the Cathedral where he had served faithfully for more than half a century. His book of *Directions* was the third work of its kind published in England; Marbeck's *Booke of Common Praier noted*, 1550, and John

[1] See Hawkins's *History of Music*, BOOK xv. ch. cxlv.

Daye's *Certaine notes*, in 1560, being the other two. Since these books nothing of the kind has been given forth by authority, and this may account for the diversity of "uses" in our several cathedrals.

The restoration of the Service marks an entirely new era in Church music in England. From this date, it may be noticed that there was a greater variety of key tonalities employed in the compositions than before. The old modes were kept in the background, if not actually discarded, and only employed for the sake of imparting an archaic effect to the music. New chord combinations were attempted, new effects suggested. A dramatic element, if the emphasis imparted to words by appropriate chords and expressive sounds may be so called, was introduced, at first sparingly, and afterwards daringly. The attempts made, not meeting with any opposition, were held to have received approval. A more sprightly form of melody was cultivated, yet the division between sacred and secular music became more marked and distinct. Music did not, however, make so rapid a progress, or develop power so quickly, that the space of difference between the music for the Church and that for the Stage, in those days the only concert-room, precluded the possibility of an occasional contact, so that the one might, under certain conditions, be taken for the other. But the resources became extended when the combinations of voices and instruments were studied and recognised as valuable and powerful factors in the sum of development. Nothing in art is of sudden appearance. No new form of ideas starts fully grown and ready armed, as Minerva is said to have originated. Everything is of slow growth, and though some things may take unexpected shapes, all can be traced to a primitive germ.

The extraordinary works of the three great geniuses in music who followed the period of the Restoration, Wise, Humfrey, and Blow, are the natural sequence of the long period of preparation which preceded them. The field of art had lain fallow during the Interregnum, and when the soil was new ploughed it gave forth abundance of fresh and vigorous forms, strengthened by the long period of unproductive rest.

It is strange that these three, the first of the Children of the Chapel after the service was restored to former uses, should have become so famous in the world of music only to be superseded by Henry Purcell, one who "coming after was preferred before them." All were children in 1660. Purcell an infant in arms, or at the best just learning to exercise independent powers of locomotion. Wise, Humfrey, and Blow not more than twelve years old each. Wise, a droll, witty, yet passionate child; Humfrey, delicate in health, but "mighty self-conceited;" and Blow, gentle, yielding and good-natured. Their master, Henry Cook, had himself been a chorister in the Chapel Royal, and when his voice changed he abandoned music for a time and entered the army. When the Rebellion broke out in 1642, he, being then about thirty years of age, obtained a captain's commission, and from that time was always afterwards distinguished by his military title. At the time when King Charles the Second ascended the throne, Cook, who had resumed the practice of music, was one of those men of the profession who, as Tom Brown says, "hung between the church and the playhouse, like Mahomet's tomb between two loadstones." He was appointed Master of the Children in 1660, and although he is by no means famous for any of his musical productions in writing, for all that they are very commendable, his merit as a teacher must have been great. Burney says that Cook composed the music for the king's coronation, but that none of his sacred music was ever printed. Anthony Wood states that he died of grief in 1672 at finding himself supplanted in reputation and favour by his pupil Pelham Humfrey. But Anthony Wood tells so many stories that are not quite true, that everything he proposes must be received with a certain reservation. Cook must have been nearly, if not over, sixty years of age at the time of his death. Men who have been soldiers, and have learned to smile at fortune's frowns, and who, like he, have enjoyed high patronage and ultimate success, do not always die of grief when near the grand climacteric. Besides, it is not easy to see the reason of any jealousy, unless it arose from a contemplation of powers he never possessed. Humfrey was esteemed because he was a composer. Cook never laid claim to much distinction as a writer. Humfrey was an excellent organist and "harpsicon" player. Cook played the lute, and enjoyed the best reputation in that capacity in his days and through all his life. Therefore, the story of the cause of his death, like many other of the pretty statements of Anthony Wood, must be taken *cum grano salis*. The words of several anthems by Cook are inserted in the second edition of Clifford's *Anthem Book*, 1664; but the music is en-tirely lost. The first edition of this work was printed in 1663, under the title of *Divine Services and Anthems, usually sang in the Cathedrals and Collegiate Choires in the Church of England*, by J. C. [James Clifford]. This was the first collection of words of anthems published in London. The compiler was born in 1622 in the parish of St. Mary Magdalen, in Oxford.[1] He was admitted as chorister in Magdalen College Chapel in 1632, and resigned in 1642, when he was in his twentieth year, but took no degree in the university. He became or-dained in 1660, and was made one of the minor canons of St. Paul's Cathedral on July 1st, 1661. "He was made senior cardinal in 1682, was also reader in the church of St. Gregory by St. Paul's near Carter Lane which is near the said cathedral, and afterwards chaplain to the Honourable Society of Sergeants' Inn, near Fleet Street, London." He died about the year 1700.

It is remarkable to note that at the time of the Re-storation there were very few English Church composers alive and at work. Matthew Lock gave his attention chiefly to music for the stage when he did write, and being a Papist would not contribute anything for the service of the Church in which he was educated but had now deserted. William Childe of Windsor was over sixty years of age, discouraged if not broken down in spirit by the long neglect of the Church's institutions, and the rapacious greed of its re-established

[1] Dr. Rimbault in his preface to *Tallis's Service*, 1845, affirmed that Clifford was a pupil of Birde's. A comparison of dates will show that this could hardly have been the case.

ministers; and Benjamin Rogers, at that time at Eton, had acquired the somewhat settled habits of a man of forty-six, and probably neglected the art of composition as he is known to have neglected his college duties.

There was no composer of note representing English ecclesiastical musical art worthier than Rogers, who might have been a great man had his industry been equal to his ability. Musical art was not dead, but it was dormant, and as the need for a supply of music fit for the wants of the Church existed and was pressing, adaptations from foreign composers were supplied for the first time. Dean Aldrich of Christ Church, Oxford, probably the first amateur of his time, was moved to an endeavour to meet this demand. There are many volumes of music from foreign authors, Palestrina, Carissimi, Vittoria, and others, with English words of his own finding, still preserved in the library of Christ Church to which he bequeathed them. He was a good scholar and a fair musician, but he was one of those clever men who spread themselves over too wide a surface to be able to cover any particular spot more than respectably. He wrote much music which has been accepted as original, but which imparts only a satellite-like reflection of the greater suns in whose light he was for ever basking. He produced an annotated edition of the Greek Classics. In distant imitation of Wren he designed three sides of the Peckwater quadrangle in his own college, built the chapel of Trinity College, and the Church of All Saints in High Street. His name is perpetuated in Oxford by a treatise on "Logic," and, in addition to the architectural monstrosities alluded to, by his passion for smoking tobacco. Out of the region of his *Alma Mater* he is remembered as the author of a service in G, written on the model of Gibbons and Tallis, and by a round, *Hark, the bonny Christ Church bells*, which finds its way persistently into cheap collections of music, but which few ever sing, or few have heard sung. His adaptations were made at a time when English Church music as represented by Humfrey, Blow, and Purcell was asserting itself in a new direction and needed all possible encouragement. The production of the works by the Italian musicians, unquestionably noble efforts, were not made with a view to their use or employment by other churches than those for which they were composed. The antique forms of music, very beautiful and imposing, which they represented, were equally well if not better displayed in the works by English writers of the sixteenth and seventeenth centuries, which it now became almost a fashion to neglect, and to dispraise in favour of everything of a foreign origin. The distrust in English musical art began from this date, and notwithstanding the fact that Henry Purcell was born, lived, laboured, and died in the space of time during which Dean Aldrich enjoyed the full maturity of his powers, the prejudice against English music was not removed by the works of our great composer, probably because Aldrich was in a position to influence those who, in turn, influenced popular opinion. Dean Henry Aldrich was born in 1646, and died in 1710.

Another clerical musician who lived at this period,

Dr. Robert Creyghton, of Wells, is remarkable for having introduced more sprightly phrases into his Church music than it had been the wont to do before. He was also credited with having written much of his music in triple measure, "the like being nowhere else to be observed in the Church writers." This is not quite correct, as there are several pieces by the older musicians in which this "time" measure is employed. Orlando Gibbons used triple measure in his services, and other pieces for sacred use. Creyghton was an excellent amateur, and had acquired considerable knowledge of music while in exile with King Charles II., but he made no new discoveries in music. He used the skill he possessed with judgment and taste, as his services and anthems show, particularly, *I will arise*, among the latter, which is in canon form. He was perhaps the first who employed the key of E flat in Church music if, as it is said, he wrote the service in that key associated with his name, soon after his appointment as Greek professor at Cambridge in 1662. He was canon and precentor of Wells Cathedral in 1674, and died at the age of ninety-seven in that city in the year 1736.

A short account of another minor light in music, Thomas Tudway, may complete this page of history. He made an attempt to collect the anthems of the old English writers at the request of Edward, Lord Harley, and succeeded in scoring as many as fill some half a dozen volumes which are now in the British Museum. It is said that he was one of those called the second set of children educated at the Chapel Royal under Dr. Blow, but the statements made concerning him do not agree the one with the other. Blow was not appointed to any place in the Chapel Royal, except that of chorister, until March, 1674, and did not hold the office of master of the boys until the death of Pelham Humfrey a few months later. Hawkins, who says that Tudway was a pupil of Blow, also says that on the 22nd of April, 1664, he was admitted to sing tenor at St. George's, Windsor. It is hardly possible that he should have grown into a child and found his treble voice again to become the pupil of Blow at the Chapel Royal. If he was at the Chapel at all, it may be assumed that he was one of the fellow-choristers of Blow, but a year or two older than he, certainly not younger. He was by no means possessed of like ability. He was appointed organist at King's College in Cambridge in 1671, three years before Blow became once more attached to the Chapel Royal. In 1681 he graduated Bachelor of Music, and in 1705, when Queen Anne visited the University, he was made Doctor, and Professor of music in succession to Dr. Staggins, the first professor of music in the University, who had held the honour since 1684. The post was at that time without emolument. Dr. Tudway was called composer and organist extraordinary to Queen Anne. The titles might have been reversed with propriety, for the two or three songs and catches, which are in print with his name attached thereto, and the multitude of his effusions which are not, prove him to have been an extraordinary composer, but without the power of extending a belief in his own genius beyond himself. Influenced by his dislike to the introduction of passages of fugal imitation in vocal music, on the ground that they obscured the sense of the words, his music is like chaff for dryness, and unlike chaff for heaviness. He was a man of little ability but of a "shrewd wit," if a passion for punning can be so distinguished. His "singular style of conversation," however, did not lose him any friends, and though it could not succeed in making him a great musician, it helped to secure for him many personal comforts and, strange to say, also a good share of the world's respect. He died in 1730. He was not accurate as an historian, for in his manuscript collection of anthems he states that one by Tallis, *Discomfit them, O Lord*, was made for the victory over the Spanish Armada in 1588, three years after Tallis was dead. He also affirms that the service in F by Gibbons was written in 1635, at which time Gibbons had been buried in Canterbury Cathedral ten years. His assertion with regard to the club anthem of Turner, Blow, and Humfrey, will be examined in the notice of the life of the latter. Thomas Tudway's chronology and the dates concerning him, seem to be capable of, if not to demand, revision.

CHAPTER IX.

MICHAEL WISE, PELHAM HUMFREY, HENRY PURCELL, JOHN BLOW, WILLIAM TURNER, JEREMIAH CLARK.

WISE, Humfrey, and Blow, were among the first set of Children of the Chapel when the service of the Church of England was restored, with the return

of King Charles in 1660.   They were all born about the
same time, 1647 or 1648, and it may be supposed that
they were selected from among others, not because they
promised to be good singers, but because they already
had had some training and were fairly well skilled in
music.   Michael Wise was born at Salisbury, and it
may be assumed that he obtained some instruction
in his early days in the Cathedral there.   At the
Chapel Royal he had the advantage of being under
Henry Cook, and of having Pelham Humfrey and John
Blow as his fellow students.[1]

Wise was nominated organist and master of the
choristers at the Cathedral in his native city in 1668,
he being then, as was supposed, in his twentieth year.
In July, 1675, he was appointed to the place of a
gentleman in the Chapel Royal, and in 1686 became
vicar-choral and almoner of St. Paul's, the latter office
carrying with it the office of master of the choristers.
King Charles was wont to favour Michael Wise, who
being appointed to attend the Royal progresses, claimed
as king's organist the privilege of playing to His
Majesty on the organ, at whatever church he went,
whether the instrument was good, bad, or of no quality
at all.   By this it may be inferred that Wise had a
great notion of the importance of his office.   He was
not an unpleasant man, according to all accounts, but
he must have been subject to fits of ungovernable
passion, one of which was unfortunately the cause of
his death.   Burney says that he was killed in a street
fray at Salisbury, by the watchmen, in 1687.   The

[1] Burney, *History of Music*, vol. iii. p. 454.

more accurate account of the matter is this: "He had quarrelled with his wife on some trivial matter, and rushed out of his house. The watchman met him while he was yet boiling with rage, and commanding him to stand and give an account of himself, he struck the guardian of the peace to the ground, who in return aimed a blow at his assailant with his bill, which broke his skull, of the consequence whereof he died." In his anthems and services Wise exhibits no little genius. Of a lively fancy and quick imagination in himself, his music reflects his disposition, not because it is lively—for as a rule, he is must successful in the expression of the sorrowful and pathetic, as in *The Ways of Zion*, and *Prepare ye the Way of the Lord*—but because of the passionate accent with which the sentiments are expressed. In the first-named anthem, the melody of the words, *For these things I weep*, and in the second, the dramatic power expressed in the duet for trebles, *And the Voice said, Cry*, is equal with anything ever attempted in the way of expression in sacred music. Written more than two hundred years ago, these passages are as fresh as if newly given forth from the brain of the most tender and expressive among modern musicians. In the generality of his compositions, not only do we find the most earnest endeavour to give in music the full meaning of particular passages, but those passages are made part of a picturesque whole, in which religious sentiment and utterance are enforced by means of beautiful melody and vivid harmony. One of the faults belonging to the age, and especially notable in his music, is the frequency with which he uses the "perfect cadence" at the conclusion of a sentence. In the works of all the Church writers before him, this seems to have been avoided, and the plagal cadence preferred. Wise probably learnt its use from Humfrey, who brought it with him from Lully, who acquired it from the study of Carissimi. It was with him as a new toy, with which he constantly played.

His fellow pupil, Pelham Humphrey, Humphreys, or Humfrey, as he occasionally signed his name, was born in 1647, and was said to be a nephew of Colonel John Humphrey, a noted Cromwellian, and Bradshaw's sword-bearer; he began to compose while he was yet a chorister, for in the second edition of Clifford's book, *Divine Services and Anthems*, 1664, there are the words of five of the anthems by Pelham Humfrey, one of the Children of His Majesty's Chapel. "The club anthem," *I will always give thanks*, so-called because it was the joint composition of Humfrey, Blow, and Turner, was probably written during these early years. Dr. Tudway, with his customary chronological inaccuracy, says it was written to celebrate a naval victory over the Dutch in 1665. This could not have been the case, for Humfrey left the choir in 1664. Turner was modest and retiring in his disposition; Humfrey, wild and quick; Blow, good-natured and conciliatory. Dr. Boyce, when he stated that the anthem was written as a memorial of friendship and fraternal esteem by the young composers, probably spoke with authority. Humfrey wrote the first part, Blow the concluding movement, and Turner the bass solo. When in the course of nature Humfrey was no longer able to sing in the choir, the ability he exhibited prompted the king to send him to France, there to improve himself under Lully. The king had already encouraged his musicians to compose anthems of a brisk and lively fashion, with symphonies and ritornells " between, to be played upon viols, cornets, and sacbuts, in the organ loft," but he rightly thought that if he could have young Humfrey educated in the mode of France, his own genius, tempered with the knowledge he could gain, would be decidedly to the augmentation of his own pleasure. Accordingly, in 1664, he was furnished with 200*l.* from the secret service money to defray the charges of his journey, and he received in the two years following, 100*l.* and 150*l.* respectively. He remained for the most of his time in Paris and studied under Lully. When he returned in October, 1667, he found he had been appointed, in his absence, to the place in the Chapel made vacant by the death of Thomas Hazzard. The new pieces he had brought with him were greatly admired, as they deserved to be. He had learnt to be skilful in the art of scoring, and his own genius had become developed, so that he was able to produce anthems which are to this day models of beauty in expression, of striking emphasis in the words, and an apt and happy union of sound and sense. Much of this must be attributed to his own genius, and perhaps something may be owing to the influence of his master, Henry Cook. Such of Cook's songs as are extant are marked by characteristic taste and expression, sufficient to serve as a pattern for sensitive boys to follow and expand, more especially those who were compelled to work, as there is no doubt Cook's boys were. His military experience would have led him to insist upon implicit obedience, and the habits of the time which made children submissive through fear to parents and superiors, compelled them to fulfil their tasks in order to avoid punishment. That these " first children of the Chapel " must have worked hard, the events of the career of each in after life tend to prove. Wise was organist of a Cathedral at the age of twenty, Humfrey a gentleman of the King's Chapel and a recognised composer at nineteen, and Blow organist of Westminster Abbey at the age of twenty-one. The story of Henry Cook dying of grief because one of his boys was successful is hard of belief. Still less credible is it that he should have felt chagrined because three of them excelled him in composition. He was, if human nature was the same then as it is now, proud of his pupils, and of his own superiority as a teacher. If he was grieved at anything, it would have been to see Master Pelham, as Pepys calls him, grown so conceited with airing the modish French ways he had acquired during his sojourn in Paris with " Master Lully, of the Grand Monarch's Chapel." Humfrey had been sent out with good credentials to the Court of France, and for the sake of his master, the King of England, who was very partial to him, he was doubtless well treated. He had been furnished with ample funds out of the secret service money, and being vain, conceited, and fond of pleasure, had improved his opportunities for cultivating his appreciation of himself. He had learned something from Lully, and as Dr. Hullah observes in his lectures on the *Transition Period of Musical,*

History, had formed his style, though at second hand, on that of Carissimi, for Lully had had the good sense or good fortune to form *his* style on that of the great Italian master; unquestionably the greatest genius of the seventeenth century. As a boy of fourteen young Humfrey had distinguished himself as a composer. Pepys, in his Diary, tells us, Nov. 22, 1663: "The anthem was good after sermon, being the fifty-first Psalme, made for five voices by one of Captain Cooke's boys, a pretty boy, and they say there are four or five of them that can do as much." This anthem is probably the one printed in Boyce's *Collection*. Once more we read, under date Nov. 1, 1667: "To chapel, it being All Hallows Day, and heard a fine anthem made by Master Pelham, who is come over." Finally, the following implied estimate of the behaviour of Master Pelham is as bright and vivid a picture of character and humour, and *vraisemblance*, as one of Barnard's book illustrations:—

"Nov. 15, 1667. Home, and there find as I expected, Mr. Cæsar and little Pelham Humfreys, lately returned from France, and is an absolute monsieur, as full of form and confidence and vanity, and disparages everything and everybody's skill but his own. But to hear how he laughs at all the king's musick here, as Blagrave and others, that they cannot time nor tune, nor understand anything; and the Grebus, the Frenchman, the king's master of the musick, how he understands nothing, nor can play on any instrument, and so cannot compose, and that he will give him a lift out of his place; and that he and the king are mighty great."

Notwithstanding his conceit, Humfrey was a man of genius, and the new forms of composition he introduced into Church music became the models for future following. To quote Dr. Hullah's words from the same work alluded to above :—

"In place of the overlapping phrases of the old masters, growing out of one another like the different members of a Gothic tower, we have masses of harmony subordinated to one rhythmical idea; in place of sustained and lofty flights we have shorter and more timorous ones, these even relieved by frequent halts and frequent divergencies; and in lieu of repetition or presentation of a few passages under different circumstances, a continually varying adaptation of music to changing sentiment of words, and the most fastidious observance of their emphasis and quantity. It would be easy to point out the faults in Pelham Humphrey's music, as in all the music of his time, but the faults were at least counterbalanced by the beauties, which were once novelties as well as beauties, and which must ever remain beauties, though to us they have lost their companion charm."

As already stated, Humfrey was appointed Gentleman of the Chapel Royal on January 24, 1666–7, and sworn into his place on the 26th October in the same year after his return from France. He became Master of the Children after Cook in 1672. In the same year, on 8th August, he was made, conjointly with Thomas Purcell, the uncle of the famous Henry, "Composer is ordinary for the violins to His Majesty," at which time he wrote several pieces for the band of "four-and-twenty fiddlers all on a row," which had been set up in imitation of "Les petits Violons" conducted in Paris by Lully, and many anthems with instrumental accompaniments, some of which are printed, but without the orchestral parts, in Boyce's collection. There are many of his anthems and services still in MS. in various cathedrals. All his compositions are notable for the expression they contain, and for many new combinations of chords not before introduced. The sharp fifth as a passing note, the major third and minor sixth on a bass note, a sequence of imperfect fifths, and the augmented, or, as it was called, the extreme sharp sixth, as well as the flat third and sharp fourth, all new to church music, were employed by him for the first time. He also indulged in "extreme keys," for he writes boldly not only in C minor but actually in F minor. It is therefore not at all inconsistent with reason to suppose that his violinists did not use fretted finger-boards on their instruments, but were able to temper their scales at will. The sound of these keys on the organs of that date would not have been pleasant.

Some of his songs were printed after his death in *Choice Ayres, Songs, and Dialogues*, 1676–84; in *Harmonia Sacra*, 1714, and other collections. He is said to have written many of the words of the songs set by the composers of his time, and to have had as "fanciful a wit as he had a delicate hand on the lute." He died at Windsor, July 14th, 1674, in his twenty-seventh year, and was buried in the cloisters of Westminster Abbey, near the south-east door.

It is sad to think that his life may possibly have been shortened by indulgence in the temptations the age offered, and which he had not the strength of will to resist. But short as his life was, perhaps shorter than that of any musician recorded in history, his genius was great, and its influence over art remarkable. His fellow-pupils, Wise and Blow, undoubtedly adopted his forms of expression and employed his discoveries. His ideas were further expounded by Croft, Weldon, Clark, and others even so late as the time of Maurice Greene. He was the first master of England's great musician, Henry Purcell.

Of this last-named genius a mere sketch must suffice, as his life and labours have been exhaustively treated by Mr. W. H. Cummings in one of the books in the series to which the present work belongs.

Purcell was born in 1658, was admitted into the Chapel Royal at the age of six years, became organist of Westminster Abbey in 1675, in his eighteenth year, and died in 1695.

John Blow, Purcell's second master, was born in 1648, at North Collingham, Nottinghamshire, a village about five miles from Newark, and eight from Southwell. It is supposed that he received the rudiments of his musical education at home, probably from some musician connected either with Southwell or Lincoln. At the age of twelve years he became one of the children of the Chapel Royal. It is not pretended that the ancient system of impressing choristers was resorted to in order to refurnish the Chapel with boys' voices, though the king's prerogative remained unimpaired, but it is possible that the best boys from various cathedral centres were selected to make

up the number required. That the musicians of
the old establishments were striving to earn a living
by the exercise of their profession is well known, even
though no vestige of the old form of worship, nor any
sort of musical service, was being performed at the
cathedrals and collegiate churches during the interregnum. It would be impossible otherwise to account
for the extraordinary ability exhibited by these "first
boys of the Chapel," if they commenced their musical
education after they had been selected, and at a
time when a disposition for work is difficult to
create. The words of certain anthems given by
Clifford, prove that young Blow's compositions were
even then considered worthy of performance; yet
when the book was published he could only have
been in his sixteenth year. It is therefore certain
that he possessed some amount of musical knowledge,
acquired in an unknown place, in an undetermined
manner, before he came to London. It has been stated
that John Hingston, organist to Oliver Cromwell, gave
young John Blow lessons upon the organ; these he
continued afterwards with Christopher Gibbons, one of
the sons of Orlando Gibbons. It then remains to
inquire was Hingston ever at Newark, Lincoln, or Southwell? If not, where could young Blow have received
instruction from him? Certain it is that, whoever
were his masters, he profited greatly by the lessons
he obtained, so much so that in 1669 he was appointed
organist of Westminster Abbey. This post he held for
eleven years, when he resigned it to make room for Henry
Purcell, his pupil. In 1674 (March 16th) he was sworn

in as gentleman of the Chapel in the place of Roger Hill, and on the death of Pelham Humfrey in the same year, was appointed master of the children. In the year 1680 he was made one of the organists of the Chapel, holding at the same time the place of organist of St. Margaret's, Westminster. He was one of the deputies at St. Paul's Cathedral, and in 1689 became Almoner and Vicar-Choral, both of which posts he is said to have resigned in 1693 in favour of Jeremiah Clark, who had been his pupil, thus for the second time yielding as it were to his own children. In 1699 the office of composer to the Chapel Royal, at the suggestion of Dr. Tillotson, at that time Dean of St. Paul's, was instituted, and Blow received the first appointment, with a salary of forty pounds a year.

Hawkins says of him, that he was " a very handsome man in his person, and remarkable for a gravity and decency in his deportment suited to his station, though he seems by some of his compositions to have been not altogether invincible to the delights of a convivial hour. He was a man of blameless morals, and of a benevolent temper; but was not so insensible of his own worth as to be totally free from the imputation of pride. Such as would form a true estimate of his character as a musician, must have recourse to his compositions for the Church, his services and anthems, which afford abundant reason to say of Dr. Blow, that among Church musicians he has few equals and scarce any superior."

There is a story related on the authority of Mr. Samuel Weely, a scholar of Blow's and of Brand's, one of the vicars-choral of St. Paul's, with reference to one of Blow's anthems. In the latter part of the year 1688, King James, having heard a composition by an Italian musician, asked Blow if he could equal it, which Blow undertook to do, and by All Saints' Day had completed the anthem, " I beheld and lo." The king sent Father Petre to express his very great approval of the composition, which message was duly delivered with an addendum of the Jesuit's own. " For myself, I think it too long." Blow, stung out of his usual gravity and decency in deportment, replied, " That is the opinion of but one fool, and I heed it not." Father Petre with malicious vengefulness prevailed upon his majesty to suspend Blow, but the flight of the king removed the suspension. Blow owed his title of doctor in music to Sancroft, Archbishop of Canterbury, and very few who have received that distinction have deserved it more. This was the only honour conferred upon him in his lifetime, unless the fact of the performance of his " Gloria Patri," to Latin words, in the Pope's chapel be true, and considered as such. Mr. Husk in his account of Blow, in Grove's Dictionary, says that Blow was a voluminous composer, his works comprise fourteen Church Services, and upwards of one hundred Anthems, nearly the whole of which are still extant, although but few are in print. They also include Sacred Songs, Duets, &c. (many of which are printed in Playford's *Harmonia Sacra*, 1688, 1714); Odes for New Year's Day, 1682, 1683, 1686, 1687, 1688, 1689, 1693 [?], 1694, and 1700; Odes for St. Cecilia's Day, 1684 [printed], 1691, and 1700, besides two which cannot

be assigned to any particular year; Ode written by
Dryden on the death of Purcell, 1695; Songs (with which
the various collections of the period abound); Catches,
(many of them printed in "The Catch-Club," The Pleasant Musical Companion, 1724, and other collections);
Organ pieces; Lessons for the Harpsichord, 1698 [printed]
and 1705 [printed with some by Purcell]. In 1700
Blow published, by subscription, a collection of his songs,
&c., under the title of *Amphion Anglicus*, with his portrait
prefixed. In the preface to this work he expressed his
intention of publishing his church music, but unfortunately never accomplished his purpose, a circumstance
much to be regretted, since it is upon those productions
that his fame chiefly rests. Three services and eleven
anthems of his are printed by Boyce. He died October
1, 1708, and was buried in the cloisters of Westminster
Abbey. On his tombstone is engraved, on an open book,
the canon set to the words of the " Gloria Patri " in his
" Gamut " service. The inscription on the monument
concludes with these words: "His own musical compositions, especially his church musick, are a far nobler
monument to his memory than any other that can be
raised for him." The truth of this statement no unpre-
judiced musician can deny.

Blow's fellow pupil, William Turner, was one among
the youngest of the first children of the Chapel, not one
of the second set, as Hawkins, and Burney who copied
from him, both state. They each say that Turner was
a pupil of Blow's, and Burney, after repeating that statement, quotes that veracious and logical historian Dr.
Tudway in manner conformable, for he says that the

Club Anthem with orchestral accompaniments written by Humfrey, Blow, and Turner, while they were fellow pupils, was composed by order of Charles the Second, at a very short notice, on account of a victory at sea over the Dutch. It is not worth while to refute this statement. The anthem exists, and was unquestionably written by the three boys, Humfrey, Blow, and Turner. The career of the two former has been traced, it only remains to add a few words concerning William Turner. His life was long, but it was placid and comparatively uneventful. When his voice broke he sang counter-tenor, and such a quality of voice being unusual if not rare, he found no difficulty in obtaining places in the Chapel Royal, Westminster Abbey, and St. Paul's Cathedral, all of which he held simultaneously, a system of pluralism permitted by the authorities, the hours at which the services were held being to some extent arranged to accommodate the singers. He was admitted Doctor of Music in the University of Cambridge by accumulation in 1696. He died on the 13th day of January, 1739-40, at the age of eighty-eight,[1] and was buried in the cloisters of Westminster Abbey, together with his wife Elizabeth, who died four days before him. They had been married nearly seventy years, and in their relation exhibited to the world an illustrious example of conjugal virtue and felicity. Their only daughter was married to John Robinson, organist of Westminster

[1] The double date 1739-40 is given in accordance with the practice of the time, arranged to accommodate both classes of the community. One, which held that the year began with the first of January, the other, which maintained that the 25th of March commenced the new year.

Abbey, and the composer of the double chant in E flat which is printed in Boyce's collection.

One of the most personally-popular musicians of his day was Jeremiah, familiarly called Jerry, Clark. He was one of Blow's pupils, and so great a favourite with his master that it is said that he vacated his place as almoner and vicar-choral at St. Paul's Cathedral in 1693, in order that Clark might be appointed. As the appointment to these offices rests entirely with the dean and chapter of the Cathedral, it is possible that there is another version of this story as yet untold. It may be that the story was made up after the circumstance that Clark was appointed to the places which Blow resigned; for deans and chapters, even in those days, were very jealous of their privileges, and would not be likely to permit any arrangement such as is here suggested. In 1695 Clark was sworn into the full place of a vicar-choral after probation, and on July 7th, 1700, he, with William Croft, received the appointment of gentleman extraordinary at the Chapel Royal, with joint reversion to the place of organist when it should fall vacant, which it did in 1704, on the death of Francis Pigott.[1] As a composer, Clark deserves a good place in the ranks of English church musicians, though his works are not numerous. His anthems, " I will love Thee, O Lord," and " Praise the Lord," are still great favourites, the one for the trustful simplicity of its pathetic sentences, the other for the quaint and lively

[1] Pigott, who for a short time—a little less than a year—had been organist of Magdalen College, Oxford, in succession to Dr. Rogers, was in his turn succeeded by Daniel, brother of Henry Purcell.

though not undignified character of its themes. He wrote many harpsichord lessons, which have been printed, some of the music for *The Island Princess*, *The World in the Moon*, and other "theatric labours," besides a number of songs scattered abroad in many collections. The grace and tenderness of his ideas often counterbalance the lack of scientific construction in his works. He is always expressive, but rarely exhibits great dignity. According to some accounts he acquired a sad and brooding disposition, and this made him take seriously to heart his rejection by a lady for whom he had formed an attachment. It is said that she was in a condition of life far above his own, and that in a passion of despair he killed himself. "Being at the house of a friend in the country, he took an abrupt resolution to return to London; his friend having observed in his manner marks of great dejection, furnished him with a horse and a servant. Riding along the road, a fit of melancholy seized him, upon which he alighted, and giving the servant his horse to hold, went into a field, in a corner whereof was a pond, and also trees, and began a debate with himself whether he should then end his days by hanging or drowning. Not being able to resolve on either, he thought of making what he looked upon as chance the umpire, and drew out of his pocket a piece of money, and tossing it into the air, it came down on its edge and stuck in the clay; though the declaration answered not his wish, it was far from ambiguous, as it seemed to forbid both methods of destruction; and would have given unspeakable comfort to a mind less disorganised than his own. Being thus interrupted in his purpose, he returned, and mounting his hòrse, rode on to London, and in a short time shot himself." The books of the vicars-choral of St. Paul's state that on "November ye first, Mr. Jerry Clarke deceased this life." The year of his melancholy death was 1707. The year of his age 38.

CHAPTER X.

WILLIAM CROFT, JOHN CHURCH, JOHN GOLDWIN, JOHN WELDON, CHARLES KING.

THE date of the death of Jerry Clark saw the dawning of a new era in musical art in England. One which, instituted independently of church music, was destined incidentally to affect it in course of time. The Church was slow to adopt the discoveries, if they may be so called, made in a new direction, until their novelty was in some sort worn off. So it arose that the secular style of the preceding half century became the ecclesiastical style of the present. This has continued to the year of grace now rolling on, and probably will endure until a further revolution in musical art takes place. It is therefore useless and needless to lament the inevitable. The new era now spoken of was commenced with the introduction of Italian opera into England, and the encouragement given to foreign productions in preference to English. Native art was almost entirely confined in its expression to church music, and out of the multitude of professors of music, composers, and performers, there are only one or two names worthy of record as having shown any disposition towards working to maintain the prestige of the name of English church composers. Weldon, Croft, Greene, and Boyce are the heroes most honourable in the list of church musicians during the first half of the eighteenth century. But there were many others worthy of the crown of parsley, if not of the bays or the olive, all having wrought well and earnestly for the cause of the art they represented, even though certain of their contemporaries were unwilling to agree that they should be so decorated.

It was not their fault if the age in which they lived was one in which true art had been left to struggle for itself, uncared for by those who ought to have cherished it; that all artistic feeling had been deadened by unsympathetic treatment. Even the sister arts of adornment and design were reduced to the expression of the barest, crudest, and most uncomely fashions not only in dress but in domestic ornament. When we contemplate the artificiality which encompassed every expression of a poetical character, it is all the greater wonder that men should have been found who were sufficiently true to their art as to be only slightly influenced by outside surroundings. The people of that age were uncertain in their loyalty, indifferent in their allegiance to the institutions of the Church, and suspicious of each other. It was therefore no happy time for musical art, which requires for its free exercise, a perfect confidence established between the giver and the receiver. Of those who

laboured for art's sake, and in the face of discourage.
ment from the Church at this date, the earliest and
perhaps the chief was William Croft. He was born at
Nether or Lower Eatington in Warwickshire, a village
about five miles from the birthplace of Shakespeare,
and only otherwise famous in history as the place at
which George Fox the quaker made his first essay at
preaching. Croft, or Crofts, as he called himself and
was sometimes called, was admitted to the Chapel
Royal as a chorister about the year 1685 under Dr.
Blow, who recommended him in 1699 to the place
of organist to the Church of St. Anne's, Soho, then
newly built. This place he kept until the year 1711,
when he resigned, and his pupil John Isham, who had
acted as his deputy from time to time, was appointed
in his place. On July 7th, 1700, he was admitted as
a gentleman extraordinary at the Chapel Royal, with
the reversion, conjointly with Jeremiah Clark, to the
organist's place, which was shared, as by agreement,
when Francis Pigott died, in 1704 [May 25]. On
the death of Clark in 1707, Croft succeeded to the
full place. In the year following, Dr. Blow, the organist
of Westminster Abbey, died, and Croft was appointed
to succeed him there. He also was appointed master
of the children and composer to the Chapel Royal at
the same time.

On July 9th he accumulated the degrees of Bachelor
and Doctor in Music at Oxford, and his exercise was
afterwards published with two odes in English and
Latin, written for the *Peace of Utrecht*, under the title
of "Musicus Apparatus Academicus." In the same

year an addition was made to the old establishment of the Chapel Royal of four gentlemen, a second composer, a lutanist, and a violist. Dr. Croft was also allowed eighty pounds a year more as master of the children, "to teach them to read, write, and to cast accompts, and to play upon the organs, and to compose music."

In the year 1724 he published, by subscription, a collection of thirty anthems and a burial-service in score, under the title of "Musica Sacra." This was the first publication of a number of anthems in score, nothing of this kind having been previously attempted, except a service of Purcell's, which does not seem to have been well done; "the faults and omissions are so gross as not to be amended but by some skilful hand." The work was in two volumes, engraved and stamped on plates, and the burial service was a completion of one begun but not finished by Henry Purcell.

In the preface to the collection, Croft states that he is "ignorant of the state of church music before the Reformation, as the same does not appear from any memorials or entries thereof in books remaining in any of our cathedral churches." Croft's anthems are full of dignity, solemnity of character, and freshness of thought, not always reaching the sublime, but never trivial or commonplace. It is true that some of his music is disfigured by the introduction of passages which recall the dance measures of the Suites or Sonatas, and are further marked by the weakness of the period—the fondness for divisions. These latter may have been introduced to accommodate Mr. Elford, a counter-tenor singer whom he praises in his preface.

His anthems, "God is gone up," "We will rejoice," among others, still hold a high place in cathedral repertories. The magnificence and power of the "Gloria" to the "Jubilate," in his service in A, has never been surpassed for point and emphasis.

There are four of Croft's anthems printed in Boyce's collection, and there are others said to be in MS. He wrote several hymn tunes, two of which, St. Anne's and St. Matthew's, will live as long as music lives. Croft wrote music for the stage, overtures and act tunes, as for example *Courtship à la Mode*, 1700; *The Funeral*, 1702; *The Twin Rivals*, 1703; *The Dying Lover*, 1704; besides sonatas or suites for the harpsichord and violin, six solos for the flute and a bass.

He died August 14th, 1727; but not, as Hawkins says, in consequence of a cold caught while attending the coronation of George II., for that monarch was not crowned until nearly two months after Croft had been buried. He lies in the north aisle of Westminster Abbey, where a monument is erected to his memory. The inscription is in Latin. Translated it reads thus: "Near to this place lies interred William Croft, Doctor in Music, organist of the Royal Chapel and of this Collegiate Church. His harmony he derived from that excellent artist in modulation who lies on the other side of him.[1] In his celebrated works, which for the most part he consecrated to God, he made a diligent progress; nor was it by the solemnity of the numbers alone, but by the force of his ingenuity and the sweetness of his manners, and even his countenance, that he

[1] This is Dr. Blow.

excellently recommended them. Having resided among mortals for fifty years, behaving with the utmost candour (not more conspicuous for any other office of humanity than a friendship and love truly paternal to all whom he had instructed), he departed to the heavenly choir on the fourteenth day of August, 1727, that, being near, he might add his own Hallelujah to the Concert of Angels. Awake up my glory, awake lute and harp, I myself will awake right early."

Croft is said to have helped Sir John Dolben, the sub-dean of the Chapel Royal, in the compilation of a book of words of anthems published in 1712, with the title of *Divine Harmony*. The like honour is also claimed for John Church, who was lay vicar and master of the choristers of Westminster Abbey, and one of the vicars-choral of St. Paul's. It is possible that both may have helped in the compilation. Church, who was born at Windsor in 1675, was admitted as a chorister in St. John's College, Oxford, in 1684. When his voice broke he is said to have been appointed one of the singing men at Christ Church. He left Oxford in June, 1697, and was admitted to the full place of a gentleman of the Chapel Royal on August 1st in that year, in the room of James Cob or Cobb. He wrote many services and anthems, some of which are still in use, and an *Introduction to Psalmody*, 1723, now become very scarce. He died January 5th, 1741, and was buried in the south cloisters of Westminster Abbey. Hawkins does not mention his name in his *History*. He gives two lines only to Thomas Wanless. This was perhaps as much as he deserves, for he endeavoured to supplant the sublime setting of the Litany of Tallis by introducing one of his own, the plain song of which was like the refrain of a ballad. His attempt was one of the instances of perverted taste which are characteristic of the period in which he lived. Wanless was born in 1676, graduated Bachelor of Music at Cambridge in 1698, was organist of York Minster, and died about 1725.

There were numerous attempts by inferior musicians to substitute for the recognised music of the Church the dross of their own devising. The quality of the music was degenerating. The stores of the Church were not always ill-supplied. There was quantity if not quality. Still there were faithful children, who sought to lay their best efforts as treasures at the service of their mother, and who seemed to be ever striving to make a distinction between their thoughts for sacred and secular music. One of these earnest and well-meaning musicians was John Goldwin, who succeeded his master, Dr. Childe, as organist at Windsor in 1697. Some of his services and anthems are printed in Boyce's collection, in Arnold's collection, and in Page's *Harmonia Sacra.* "I have set God," in Boyce, is melodious, earnest, and pleasing. There are some "lessons" of his in MS. which are bright and of a more advanced character than his sacred music. He died in 1719. Another was John Weldon, despite what Dr. Burney says of him, namely, that "his productions appear flimsy after those of Croft's." Posterity does not seem inclined to endorse his opinion, nor can the faithful historian confirm it. John Weldon wrote some exceedingly beautiful music for the Church, in which deep religious sentiment seems to have been his motive power. It is true he does not appear to have been able to free himself from the fashions of his time ; no man can, not even the greatest genius that ever was inspired. There is always some trick of expression, some form of utterance which identifies a man's work with the age in which he lived and breathed. One method, called a "Rosalia," was common to musicians in Weldon's day ; used in descending passages it was held to typify depression, in ascending passages, exaltation. Burney states that "it is a vice of which composers of small resources are often inadvertently guilty." If, according to the same authority, the "eternal repetition of the same poor passage" be an evidence of poverty of invention, what would he have said of the thirteen reiterations of the scale passage in Mozart's "Non più andrai"? Further, what would he have thought of Wagner's music, in which repetitions are employed with what we poor moderns are inclined to think is a good effect?

In defiance of the opinion of Dr. Burney, musicians of the present day hold that the man who could write such anthems as "Hear my crying," "In Thee, O Lord" (despite the duet, "Bow down Thine ear," for alto and bass, which, in consequence of the manner in which it is occasionally sung by half-educated singers, is irreverently called the "Bow-wow duet"), "O God, Thou hast cast us out," and "Who can tell how oft he offendeth"—all of which are in common use to this day, as well as a large number which are only occasionally heard—must have been possessed not only of genius but of a sincerely religious frame of mind, such as ought to be brought to bear in the construction of music intended for continuous use in the church. These anthems, with one or two others, are for the most part independent of the fashion of the time when they were written, and though tinged by method of diction and manner of handwriting, so to speak, they will continue to live. There is evidence also that Weldon was an original thinker in music. In the anthem " Hear my crying," which even Burney acknowledges to be a pleasing and masterly composition, the six-part writing is remarkable for its freedom and melodiousness, and in the concluding movement there is the earliest instance on record of the employment of an inversion of the chord of the augmented sixth. These sixths are of the family called, alternately, German, Italian, and Neapolitan, because they were discovered by an Englishman, and that Englishman John Weldon, whose " powers of invention and harmonical combination seem very much limited."[1]

Weldon was born at Chichester about the year 1679. He was educated in the choir at Eton under John Walter, and is supposed to have been transferred to Westminster Abbey, for he was a pupil of Henry Purcell. He was appointed organist of New College, Oxford, in 1698, and left there in 1700-1 (January 6th) to become a gentleman extraordinary of the Chapel Royal. He succeeded Dr. Blow as organist in 1708. When the places of second composer in ordinary, lutanist, and violist were made in 1715, Weldon received the first-named appointment. His initial composition in

[1] Burney's *History of Music*, vol. iii. p. 613.

his new capacity was a setting of the Prefaces, "Sanctus" and "Gloria," for the Communion Service, the first which had been made to those words since the days of Gibbons. Weldon also held the appointment of organist at St. Bride's Church, Fleet Street, London, and also that of St. Martin's in the Fields, in 1726, given it is said out of compliment to the King, whose organist he was. The King had been elected churchwarden to the parish, and growing tired of his office after a service of two months, gave the parish an organ which cost £1,500 by way of solace for relinquishing his duties.

Weldon wrote very little secular music. There are some single-sheet songs by him, printed at the end of the seventeenth or beginning of the eighteenth centuries, in the *Mercurius Musicus*, as well as separately, and some three collections of songs "perform'd at the Consort in York Buildings, and at y* Theatre, as also Symphony Songs for Violins and Flutes, never before Publish'd, Carefully corrected by y* Author," which were printed in score and published by Walsh. He also wrote the music for Congreve's masque, *The Judgment of Paris*, for which he obtained the first of four prizes out of a sum of two hundred pounds "subscribed by several persons of quality for the best composition on this subject."

About the year 1720 Weldon published his *Divine Harmony ; six select Anthems for a voice alone, with a Thorow-Bass for the Organ, Harpsicord, or Arch-lute.* There is in this book a picture representing the interior of St. James's Chapel during the performance of Divine Service, in which the violists, lutanists, and "Hoboy players" are performing left-handed. These anthems were written for Mr. Richard Elford, whom Dr. Croft praises so highly. Weldon died in the year 1736, and was buried in the grave-yard of St. Paul's, Covent Garden, the resting-place of many who in their lives were distinguished in literature and art. The stone which once marked the place of his burial has been removed.

Charles King, whom Dr. Greene—at first one of his boys, and afterwards one of his colleagues in St. Paul's Cathedral—was wont in jocular style to call a " very serviceable man," in allusion to the number of services he had written, next claims notice according to chronological order. He was born in 1684, was admitted as a chorister of St. Paul's in his seventh year just before Dr. Blow resigned, so he earned the right to call himself, and be called, a pupil of the famous doctor. He took the degree of Bachelor in Music at Oxford in 1704, and was appointed deputy in St. Paul's through the kind offices of Jeremiah Clark, whose sister he afterwards married. He succeeded to the place of Almoner and master of the boys on the death of Jeremiah Clark in 1707, but was not sworn in as vicar choral until October 31st, 1730. At this time he held the place of organist at the church of St. Benet Fink, by the Royal Exchange. Several of his anthems and services have been printed. There is no depth of thought in any of King's music, and its continued employment in these days is due to the fact that it is what Dr. Greene described it to be, "serviceable." He died March 17th, 1748. He was very much liked for his personal character. The tradition handed down by the boys of St. Paul's Cathedral concerning him was that—

> "Indulgence ne'er was ask'd in vain ;
> He never smote with stinging cane ;
> He never stopp'd the penny fees ;[1]
> His boys were let do as they please."

No let seemed to be placed upon their employment of grammar if this be true.

CHAPTER XI.

MAURICE GREENE, JAMES KENT, CHARLES STROUD, JOHN TRAVERS, WILLIAM BOYCE.

AFTER the deaths of Croft and Weldon, Maurice Greene rose to the front rank of the profession, and became the recognised head of English musicians. He was the third son of the Rev. Thomas Greene, D.D., vicar of the united parishes of St. Olave Jewry, and St. Martin's, Ironmonger Lane, and was born in 1695. He was admitted as a chorister in St. Paul's Cathedral in 1706, while Jeremiah Clark was yet master, and the first time he was permitted to wear his surplice was when Queen Anne visited the Cathedral in that year. Charles King

---

[1] The "penny fees" probably allude to the allowance made in old times to the choristers of St. Paul's of a penny a day out of the Almonry Fund, which the master occasionally stopped for bad behaviour. The payment has been for some years discontinued.

became master in 1707, and Greene received his first lessons in harmony under him. In 1710 he was articled for five years to Richard Brind, organist of the Cathedral. On the completion of his term he was appointed organist of St. Dunstan's in the West, chiefly through the interest of his uncle, Sergeant Greene. In 1717, Greene was appointed organist of St. Andrew's, Holborn, over the head of Daniel Purcell. He retained both situations until 1718, when he resigned them to become organist of St. Paul's on the death of his master, Richard Brind. The Dean, Dr. Godolphin, conferred upon him the place of a vicar-choral in augmentation of his stipend as organist. He was, therefore, the first vicar-choral who did not sing.

Greene was appointed organist and composer to the Chapel Royal on the death of Dr. Croft in 1727, and three years later he was invited to accept the post of professor of music at Cambridge on the death of Dr. Tudway. For this purpose he accumulated the degrees of Bachelor and Doctor in Music. His exercise, a setting of Pope's *Ode for St. Cecilia's Day*, was performed on July 6th, 1730. Pope altered the poem at Greene's request, and introduced a new stanza commencing, "Amphion thus bade wild dissensions cease." Five years later Dr. Greene was made "Master of the King's Musick" in the place of John Eccles, and as part of his duty, wrote several birthday odes, some to the wonderful words of Colley Cibber, the perverter of Shakespeare.

Greene published his *Forty Select Anthems* in 1743: these, Burney says, "are deficient in that dignity and solemnity which are essential in all compositions for the Church;" and a writer in the *Harmonicon* fifty years later, when the anthems had had a full and fair trial, states, "they combine the science and vigour of our earlier writers with the melody of the best German and Italian masters who flourished in the first half of the eighteenth century." There are other anthems published later, and many still remaining in MS. Greene also wrote a number of songs, many of which are remarkable for the grace of their melody; so that the story told of Handel, that he hung some volumes of Greene's music out of window because he said " they wanted air," can scarcely be said to be *ben trovato*, even if it was *vero*! Greene was too anxious to minister to the popular fancy of his time, and therefore much of his work is of little value. There are sufficient indications of genius in his music, to lead to the belief that he would have laboured better had he courted Art rather than fashion.

His compositions further comprised a Service in C written at Farnham in 1737; *Jephtha*, an oratorio, 1737; a pastoral to words by Dr. John Hoadley called *Florimel*, dated 1737; the *Force of Truth*, oratorio, 1744; the *Song of Deborah and Barak*, 1732; the *Judgment of Hercules*, masque, 1740. Dr. Greene also set a festival Te Deum in D with Orchestra for the service in commemoration of the suppression of the Scottish rebellion in 1745; composed *Phœbe*, a pastoral, 1748; music to Spenser's *Amoretti*, with several cantatas, many organ voluntaries, harpsichord lessons, catches and canons.

Handel being very fond of the old Father Smith organ at St. Paul's, played on it frequently, and Greene is said to have cultivated the friendship of **the** giant Saxon with a degree of assiduity that bordered on servility, but when Handel learned that he **was** equally civil to his rival, Bononcini, he would have nothing to say to him. For all Greene's admiration for Handel's genius, his works show no trace of his ever having copied any trick of thought or expression now known as Handelian. In fact, for all the evidence Greene's music may give, it may be said that musicians had not then begun to copy Handel. In the disputes between the two operatic rivals Greene is said to have behaved with great duplicity. He was a member of the Academy of Ancient Music, and with a view to exalt the character of Bononcini, produced in the year 1728 a madrigal, "In una siepe ombrosa," which gave rise to a dispute which terminated in the disgrace of his friend, for the madrigal was proved to have been written by Lotti, and not by Bononcini. Bononcini's disgrace arose from his having been found out. If Handel's thefts from other composers had been discovered he might have suffered the same fate as his rival. Dr. Greene, not able to submit to the reproaches or endure the slights of those who had marked and remembered his pertinacious behaviour in this business, left the Academy, and drew off with him the boys of St. Paul's Cathedral, and some other persons, his immediate dependents; and fixing on the great room, called the Apollo, at the Devil Tavern, in Fleet Street, for the performance of a concert, under his sole management, gave occasion to the saying, "that Dr. Greene was gone to the devil."

Dr. Greene's organ playing was greatly admired, yet he was the first who indulged in that peculiar form of playing represented by the " Cornet voluntaries"; that is to say, a habit of flourishing with a solo stop on the right accompanied with soft foundation stops on the left hand, and not always a substratum of pedal passages.

His later years were spent in comparative affluence, for his uncle, Sergeant Greene, left him an estate worth £700 a year. He gave up his teaching, and spent the greater part of his leisure in collecting and arranging the Services and Anthems of the old Church composers, copying the several parts into score, and adding a figured bass, with the intention of publishing the result of his labours. This he never carried into effect, for he died before he had completed his task, and was buried in the vault of the Church of St. Olave, Old Jewry, on December 10th, 1755, aged 60. He bequeathed his materials and work to Dr. Boyce, with a request that the latter would complete what he had begun. This was accomplished with the assistance of James Kent of Winchester. Greene left one daughter, who was married to the Rev. Michael Festing, of Wyke Regis, Dorsetshire, the son of his friend Michael Christian Festing, with whom he was associated in the foundation of the Royal Society of Musicians.

In personal appearance Greene was small of stature, and disfigured by a deformity. His courteous manners and polished address made him acceptable and welcome in society, where his natural defects were overlooked or not thought of.

Neither Hawkins nor Burney in their several Histories

seem to have had very high opinions of Dr. Greene, either personally or artistically. They each had opportunities of being acquainted with him, and their testimony may be considered to have some value when sifted from the mixture of prejudice. One seems to find fault with his character, the other with his music. Neither have they many words of praise or blame to spare for James Kent, organist of Winchester Cathedral, who assisted Dr. Boyce in the compilation of his *Cathedral Music*, and who was one of the sincerest flatterers of his master Dr. Croft. Him he not only imitated, but actually copied, and not him alone, but others, where he thought he could not be detected. Some notice may be vouchsafed to Kent's works in consequence of the extraordinary favour with which they were at one time, and still are, in some places, regarded. His greatest admirers, if they were honest, were compelled to admit, that he " followed closely the style of Dr. Croft," that "we sometimes observe in his works what may be thought to border upon conceit," or, that he " often without hesitation or scruple followed the ideas of his master in his compositions." The secret of his success lay not so much in the excellence of his music, as in the choice of words he had made. They were appropriate to certain of the seasons of the Church otherwise unprovided with music, and the usefulness of the words blinded men to the plagiarisms of the music. In some cases, the modern fashion of ignoring the works of the old English Church Composers is a manifest injustice ; there would be stern justice in ignoring Kent.

The particulars of his life are few. He was born at

Winchester on the 13th March, 1700. He was at first a chorister in the Cathedral of that city, under Vaughan Richardson, the composer of "O how amiable," and afterwards went to London, where, at the Chapel Royal, he had the advantage of being a pupil of Dr. Croft—an advantage he never failed to parade. His master recommended him to the patronage of Dr. Dolben, the Sub-dean of the Chapel, who was Croft's intimate friend. Through that patronage he became in 1717 organist at Finedon, in Northamptonshire, the seat of the Dolben family. This place he left in 1731 to become organist of Trinity College, Cambridge. Here he remained until 1737, when he was appointed to Winchester Cathedral, and held the post nearly forty years, dying in the city of his birth in the year 1776, on May 6th.

Kent had not a tithe of the genius of his fellow chorister at the Chapel Royal, Charles Stroud, whose beautiful anthem "Hear my prayer," supplicatory and pathetic, inspired Kent with more than one idea for his anthem to the same words. This marvellous boy, for he was only sixteen when he died in 1720, had he lived and carried out the promise of his infancy which this his only piece of work held out, would doubtless have been a second Purcell.

John Travers, born about the year 1707, may be spoken of in this place. He was a chorister in St. George's Chapel, Windsor, and was employed in a like capacity at Eton College, the custom then existing for the members of one choir to serve in the other. When his voice broke he commenced a course of study under Dr. Greene of St. Paul's, Dr. Godolphin, the Dean of that church, who was also Provost of Eton, paying the needful expenses for his education. The first appointment Travers obtained was that of organist of St. Paul's, Covent Garden, in 1725, a post which he held conjointly with that of Fulham parish church. Upon the decease of Jonathan Martin in 1737, Travers was appointed organist to the Chapel Royal, where he remained until his death in 1758, when he was succeeded by Dr. Boyce.

The Service in F, and one or two of his anthems which are still in use, such as "Keep, we beseech Thee," and "Ascribe unto the Lord," are grave in style, but with less pretension to solemnity than solidity. They are all contrapuntal in character, and have many of the harshnesses of "ingenious contrivance." His canzonets are written in an entirely different vein. They are eighteen in number, to words many of which were written by Matthew Prior, and exhibit a charm and grace of melody which even now commands admiration from those who hear them, all old-fashioned as they are in general texture. He also published *The Whole Book of Psalms, for one, two, three, four, and five voices, with a thorough-bass for the harpsichord.*

Travers was said to have been learned in the literature of music, and to have practised the art of composition with Dr. Pepusch. He did not give to the world any of the results of his studies in literature; and Burney hints that the consequence of his labours with Dr. Pepusch was that "his compositions, however fine the harmony, can only be ranked with pieces of mechanism, which labour alone may produce without the assistance of genius;"—a well-turned sentence, tinged with the malice of untruth.

William Boyce, whose name and labours have found frequent mention in the preceding pages, was born in London in 1710, at Joiners' Hall, Upper Thames Street. His father was beadle of the company, and a cabinet maker. Young Boyce at an early date exhibited a taste for music, and he was admitted as a chorister of St. Paul's Cathedral by Charles King, then master of the children. When he left the choir he was articled to Dr. Greene, who obtained for him the place of organist of Oxford Chapel, Vere Street, in 1734. He became acquainted with Dr. Pepusch and was a constant visitor at his houses in Bartlett's Buildings and in Boswell Court. In 1736 John Weldon died, and Boyce succeeded him as composer to the Chapel Royal; in the same year he became organist of St. Michael's Church, Cornhill, in the place of Thomas Kelway who went to St. Martin's in the Fields, at which time also he resigned Oxford Chapel. As composer to the Chapel Royal he now began to write many of the fine anthems which were published after his death. In the year 1737 he was appointed conductor of the Festival of the three choirs, Gloucester, Worcester, and Hereford, a post he held until 1745. In 1740 he wrote the music of an oratorio, *David's Lamentation over Saul and Jonathan*, words by John Lockman, which was performed at Covent Garden Theatre. In the year following he wrote two odes for St. Cecilia's Day, one by the Rev. Mr. Vidal, "The charms of harmony display," another by Lockman, "See fam'd Apollo and the Nine." "The Serenata of

Solomon," words by Edward Moore, was produced in 1743; one of itt songs "Softly rise, O southern breeze," with bassoon obbligato, is not yet forgotten. Boyce was elected organist to the church of Allhallows, Thames Street, in 1749, and in the same year he took his degree as Doctor in Music at Cambridge. His exercise, an anthem, "O be joyful in God," and an ode to words by William Mason, M.A., written for the installation of the Duke of Newcastle as Chancellor of the University, were given at that time—the anthem with orchestral accompaniment in St. Mary's Church, and the ode in the Senate House. Boyce also wrote the music for Lord Lansdowne's "Masque of Peleus and Thetis," and that for an entertainment by Moses Mendez called "The Chaplet," which was succeeded in the following year, 1750, by another called "The Shepherd's Lottery." In 1755 Boyce succeeded Dr. Greene as master of the King's band of music, as well as conductor of the Festivals of the Sons of the Clergy annually held in St. Paul's. It was part of his duty as composer to the King to set the birthday odes of the Poets Laureate of that time—first Colley Cibber, whom Johnson thought "by no means a blockhead," and then William Whitehead—

> "—his worth a pinch of snuff,
> But for a Laureat,—he was good enough."

As conductor of the Festivals of the Sons of the Clergy he made some additional accompaniments to Purcell's Te Deum and Jubilate in D, which were performed on those occasions for many years afterwards. In 1758 John Travers died, and Boyce was appointed to the place of organist at the Chapel Royal, and then resigned St. Michael's, Cornhill, and Allhallows. At this time also, the infirmity of deafness, which had troubled him more or less from his earliest youth, became so strong as to compel him to give up teaching. He then turned his attention to the bequest of Dr. Greene, and began to arrange the materials which had been collected, himself making many additions, acquired it is said by his intercourse with Dr. Pepusch. This work was published in three volumes, under the title of *Cathedral Music*, the first in 1760, the last in 1778, only a year before his death. The sale was not remunerative, but the fame of Boyce as a cathedral musician has been greatly exalted by the publication, inasmuch as it proved his high appreciation of the works of his great predecessors in the Church.

He died on February 7th, 1779, in consequence of a fit of the gout from which he had long suffered. He was buried in the crypt under the centre of the dome of St. Paul's Cathedral. His widow published in 1780 a volume containing *Fifteen Anthems and a Te Deum and Jubilate*, and in 1790 a second volume, edited by Dr. Philip Hayes, was given to the world. These volumes are generally known to cathedral men as " Boyce's Own," in contradistinction to " Boyce's Collection." This last-named work was reprinted from the original plates in 1788, with a portrait and memoir of Boyce by Ashley, who had purchased the work. Modern editions of the collection were published by Joseph Warren and Vincent Novello, the latter also giving to the world many anthems by Boyce not before printed. Boyce wrote

music for Dryden's *Secular Masque*, 1745; twelve
Sonatas for two violins and bass, 1747; a Concerto;
eight Symphonies; "An Ode to Charity," which
contains the duet "Here shall soft Charity repair," so
long popular; a paraphrase of part of Pindar's first
Pythian Ode, 1749; masque in *The Tempest*; dirge in
Cymbeline; dirge in *Romeo and Juliet*; trio in *The
Winter's Tale*; two odes in Home's tragedy, *Agis*,
1758; besides many songs which appeared in the
British Orpheus, *The Vocal Musical Mask*, the *Lyra
Britannica*, and other books. Among his songs the
perennial "Heart of Oak," with Garrick's words, must
not be forgotten.

Boyce wrote a Service in A, Te Deum, and Jubilate,
continued by Arnold in the same key, with verse
services in A, in C, in E minor, and in G.

There is a doubt about the right of Boyce to the
anthem "O give thanks," for eight voices, which was
published in the second "Collection" edited by
Philip Hayes. In a work called the "*Cathedral
Magazine, or Divine Harmony*; being a collection of
the most valuable and useful anthems in score," 3
vols., published in 1769, the anthem is there attributed to Croft. The *Cathedral Magazine* was tolerably
well known as one of a series of publications of
expired copyright works. Greene's and Croft's anthems
were published in this series. It is therefore possible
that it was transcribed by Boyce, at the time he was
engaged in the compilation of his *Cathedral Music*.
There is no record of any steps being taken to assert
his right to the anthem, if it was his. It is a very fine

piece of music, and there is evidence elsewhere to prove that it was written by Croft.

Boyce's style, as expressed in his Church music, is massive, dignified, and impressive. In what is now called picturesque writing he was probably without a rival. His anthems " Give the King thy judgments," with its noble concluding chorus, " All kings shall fall down;" "Wherewithal shall a young man," and, above all, " O where shall wisdom be found," are as good as anything in the whole repertory of cathedral music. Like his master Dr. Greene, Boyce was a great admirer of Handel's works, and also, like his master, he never copied Handel. Even in the present, when his anthems are performed (not so frequently as they might be), their simple and pious eloquence reaches the heart of the worshipper, and stirs it to a depth of emotion that is never attained by the organ solos with vocal accompaniments which now to a great extent do duty for services and anthems in the Church.

Boyce was one of the last of a race of English Church composers possessed of power and individuality of character sufficiently marked and well set as to enable them to resist certain meretricious influences from without. Most of those that followed in the next generation seemed to be moved to utter second-hand thoughts in a second-hand manner, so that in sheer despair of obtaining anything that might be counted as truly worthy of the service of the Church, men looked abroad, and instead of studying to make themselves equal to the effort of continuing the traditions of the elders, tinged with more modern knowledge, they set themselves to work to adapt compositions not originally intended for Church use, to words that might give a colourable pretext for their introduction into church—even madrigals were arranged to words from the Bible and Prayer Book. Mr. Pitt of Worcester, Mr. Pratt of Cambridge at a little later date, and one or two others of still less authority, did much mischief in this direction by fostering a taste for the insipidly pretty in Church music in the place of the worthy, the noble, and the devotional.

CHAPTER XII.

WILLIAM HAYES, PHILIP HAYES, JAMES NARES, WILLIAM JACKSON OF EXETER, THOMAS SAUNDERS DUPUIS, JOHN JONES, BENJAMIN COOKE, JONATHAN BATTISHILL.

THE one name which represents the exception at this period is that of William Hayes, who at the outset of his career wrote several anthems which are serious and not undignified. There is no attempt at newness of thought or expression in any, and they are simply pleasing because they are not offensive. In his later days he set tunes to a number of metrical Psalms which show the effect of outside apathy in Church music, for they are evidently designed to gratify the ear, without seeking to penetrate the mind, or what was perhaps of greater importance, without occupying too much time in performance. He was born in Gloucester in the year 1707, and became a chorister of the cathedral, and in time was articled to Hine, one of the authors of the co-operative service in E, known as " Hall and Hine." In 1729 he was appointed organist at St. Mary's Church, Shrewsbury, shortly after a new organ had been erected there by Harris and Byfield. Here he remained for about two years, when he left for Worcester Cathedral. He held this appointment until 1734, and succeeded Mr. Hecht as organist of Magdalen College, Oxford. He matriculated as a member of the University on June 12th, 1735, and took his degree as Bachelor of music on July 8th in the same year. On January 14th, 1741–2, he was elected to the office of Professor of Music in succession to Mr. Goodson, deceased. Upon the opening of the Radcliffe Library, April 14th, 1749, he was honoured with a doctor's degree, upon which occasion Dr. Bradley the Savilian professor of astronomy who presented him, made an elegant Latin speech, in which he extolled him " as a man eminent in his faculty, and one whose sweetness of temper vied with that of his art."

" After a paralytic stroke, which he bore with Christian resignation for nearly three years, in a tottering state, more decayed in health than in his faculties, he resigned his breath to Him who had bestowed it, in July 1777, in his 70th year." Thus wrote his son Philip Hayes, who succeeded him as organist of Magdalen College, and also as Professor of Music in the University.

Dr. Hayes the elder gained three prizes in 1763 offered by the Catch Club for two poems and a glee —*Alleluyia*, *Miserere Nobis*, and " Melting Airs." In the same year he was appointed conductor of the Festival at Gloucester, his native place. His compositions were twelve "arietts" or ballads, and two cantatas, 1735: "Ode to the Passions," to words by William Collins, performed at Gloucester in 1760; Vocal and Instrumental music in three parts, containing, (1) the overture and songs in the *Masque of Circe;* (2) a sonata, or trio, and songs of different kinds, viz. ballads, airs, and cantatas; (3) an ode, being part of an exercise prepared for a bachelor's degree published in 1742, besides catches, glees, and canons; instrumental accompaniments to the Old Hundredth Psalm for the Festival of the Sons of the Clergy, sixteen psalms from the Rev. Mr. Merrick's version; and Cathedral music in score, written in 1745, and published by his son after his death. There are one or two other anthems of his, still in MS., in the books of Magdalen College and elsewhere. Dr. Hayes was also the author of some *Remarks on Mr. Avison's Essay on Musical Expression,* 1762.

What the father did insensibly, the son, Philip Hayes, seems to have done deliberately, for many of such of his anthems as are known are of the most trivial, commonplace, and *ad captandum* character. Of his eight anthems published, only one, "The Lord Descended," descends to posterity. His sixteen psalms written in imitation of his father are not remembered even in his old college. His oratorio, *Prophecy,* remains in MS., and several other of his works have proved to be ephemeral. He was of enormous size, and nearly equal in weight to Bright, the heavy miller of Maldon, in Essex. In good humour and appearance he was a complete representation of Shakespeare's fat knight, Sir John Falstaff. He had the reputation of being a clever player. It is certain that he was a man of taste; he collected pictures, as well as portraits of great musicians, several of which he gave to the music school at Oxford. He was born at Oxford in 1738, graduated Mus. Bac. in 1763, became Doctor in 1777, a few months after his father's death, and about a fortnight after he had been elected Professor of Music.

He was admitted to the Chapel Royal on Nov. 30th, 1767. He was organist of New College, 1776, and of St. John's College, 1790, in addition to his other appointments. He edited the *Harmonica Wiccamica*, a series of Latin sentences set to music and sung at the annual meetings of old Wykehamists in London; and some *Memoirs of Prince William Henry, Duke of Gloucester, from his birth, July 24, 1689, to October, 1697*; published in 1789. Phil Hayes, or "Fill Chaise," as he was called in reference to his bulk, died in London, March 19th, 1797, in his fifty-eighth year, and was buried in St. Paul's Cathedral.

Of the other musicians, who by reason of priority of birth ought to have been mentioned before Dr. Philip Hayes, a few words only are necessary.

John Alcock, born in London April 11th, 1715, was a chorister of St. Paul's under Charles King. Before his voice broke, at the age of fourteen, he became the pupil of Stanley, the blind organist, at that time two years his senior. In 1735 Alcock was organist at Plymouth; in 1742 he was at Reading, when he published six suites of lessons and six songs; and in 1749 we find him at Lichfield Cathedral, when he published some Concertos and psalm-tunes. On June 6th, 1755, he graduated at Oxford as Mus. Bac., and six years later proceeded to the degree of Doctor. He had resigned his place as organist in the Cathedral of Lichfield a year before, in consequence of suffering from the pains of rheumatism induced by playing in the damp, neglected church. He retained the post of lay vicar. He published a service in E Minor, a long time very popular, some anthems, and some glees, all of which are forgotten. He died at Lichfield, in March, 1806, aged ninety-one. Alcock was one of the few musicians who saw the need of making an effort to retain the supremacy of old English Church music, by avoiding the fascination of ministering to a passing popular taste, and by continuing to observe the patterns left by the old masters. He was the link between the old world and the new, less by reason of his style of writing than by the musical memories of a long life.

The next writer in order of succession was James Nares. He was born at Hanwell, Middlesex, in 1715, was admitted chorister at the Chapel Royal, under Bernard Gates, and when he was able to play the organ was appointed deputy for Pigott, of St. George's Chapel, Windsor, and became organist at York Minster in 1734. He succeeded Greene as organist and composer to the Chapel Royal in 1756, and in the same year was made Doctor of Music at Cambridge. He was appointed master of the children of the Chapel Royal in 1757 on the death of Gates. This post he resigned in 1780, and he died in 1783 (February 10th), and was buried in St. Margaret's Church, Westminster. His publications were *Eight Sets of Harpsichord Lessons*, 1748; *Two Harpsichord Lessons*, 1758; *Three Easy Harpsichord Lessons*, 1760; and *A Treatise on Singing*, which, with a *Second Treatise*, containing some duets, were the standard works employed for solfeggio purposes for the boys at the Chapel Royal and St. Paul's until some thirty years ago. He also was the author of *Il Principio; or a Regular Introduction to Playing on the Harpsichord or Organ*, which was the first instruction book based upon a progressive plan; *The Royal Pastoral; A Dramatic Ode; Collection of Catches, Canons, and Glees; Six Organ Fugues; Twenty Anthems*, 1778; *Morning and Evening Service, with Six Anthems, with a Portrait of the Composer, ætat Sixty-five*, prefixed. Nares, as judged by his music, is a very indifferent composer. He had the reputation of being an excellent trainer of boys' voices, many of his anthems having been written to exhibit the accomplishments of his young *proteges*. The degree of excellence the boys attained was not won in those days without the infliction of much corporal punishment.

The English Church composers of this period who are yet to be mentioned, are Jackson, Dupuis, and Jones. The first contributed a service in F to the stores of cathedral music; it stands as a striking example of the degeneracy of the mental power of one of the successors of Tallis, Gibbons, and Purcell. The works of either of the former, compared with either of the latter, will demonstrate the utter decadence of the art of music in the Church, as represented by the musicians of two ages, equally in repute in their time.

William Jackson, usually called Jackson of Exeter, was born in that city in 1730, where his father was a grocer. He became, in 1748, a pupil of John Travers, in London; returning to his native city to earn his living as a teacher. In 1755 he published some songs, which became exceedingly popular. His canzonets were deservedly admired, for they are full of bright and pleasing melody. He has a reputation as a Church composer, but it is based on the feeble production alluded to above. He wrote some cathedral music, which was published in 1820 by James Paddon, organist of Exeter Cathedral, and died July 12th, 1803.

Thomas Saunders Dupuis was best known to his contemporaries as an organ-player, he being one of the most skilful performers of his time. He was born of an old Huguenot family in 1733, and was a fellow-pupil of Jackson of Exeter, under Travers, having been previously one of "Mr. Bernard Gates's Boys." Dupuis was made organist to the Chapel Royal in 1779 after the death of Dr. Boyce, and in 1790 he took the degree of Doctor of Music at Oxford by accumulation. He died in 1796. A year after his death his friend and pupil, John Spencer, published his *Cathedral Music in Score*, in three volumes, the third volume containing a separate organ part to the former two, and a portrait of the composer. Of the forty-seven anthems known to have been written by Dr. Dupuis, not one has been performed at St. Paul's Cathedral for thirty-five years. At the Chapel Royal they are very rarely done, and the chief knowledge of their existence is derived from the record of the words to which they are set being retained in some books of words of anthems. Not a note of his music has been reprinted by modern publishers, with the exception of a chant or two which have found their way into collections of such pieces. By these chants the name of Dupuis is alone kept from the oblivion into which it has undeservedly fallen, for his Church music is by no means deficient in expression or force.

The next name, that of John Jones, is literally sustained upon one chant, which, when Haydn heard it in 1791, on the occasion of his visit to the festival of the Charity Children in St. Paul's, he declared that "no music had for a long time affected me so much as that innocent and reverential strain."

John Jones, born about the year 1732, could not have been a mean performer, even if he was a poor composer, for he was appointed, according to merit, as organist of the Middle Temple in 1749, " he being yet in his teens." He succeeded Dr. Pepusch, his master, as organist of the Charterhouse in 1753, and on the death of Dr. Greene, in 1755, became organist of St. Paul's, obtaining also the place of vicar-choral which Dean Godolphin had attached to the appointment. The only publication connected with his name is *Sixty Chants, Single and Double,* many of which are partly in unison, like the one which carries his name to posterity. They are nearly all distinguished by florid melodies and indifferent harmonies, and above all by a perfect disregard of the principles which should guide the construction of tunes for chanting; such for instance as employing a note of medium pitch for the reciting phrases, and keeping the compass of the melody within moderate limits. Jones died February 17th, 1796, and was succeeded at St. Paul's by an earnest, conscientious, and highly gifted musician, Thomas Attwood.

Two other musicians, contemporary with the above-mentioned, to whom posterity has been more kind if not more just, Benjamin Cooke and Jonathan Battishill, may be mentioned as instances of solid, sterling composers, not altogether unmoved by the waves of popular fancy, but at the same time not carried wholly away with the drift of the current into the unrecognisable silt. Cooke was an eminent musician and an earnest student, expert as a player, successful as a teacher, and not altogether devoid of scientific power as a composer. The Canon three in one, by augmentation, which is engraved on his tomb in Westminster Abbey, was intended by the author to be sung as an appendix to Birde's *Non Nobis*, and the subject is so cleverly chosen, and the treatment so masterly, that it is no unmeet associate with the work of his illustrious Elizabethan predecessor.

Benjamin Cooke, the son of a music publisher in Covent Garden, of the same name, was born in the year 1734. After receiving some instruction from Dr. Pepusch, he was so well qualified in a short time as to be able to act as deputy for John Robinson, the son-in-law of Dr. Turner, at Westminster Abbey. His early success inspired him with a sort of conceit which never left him through life—a conceit which prompted him to expect others to do as much as he was able to do at the like age. It is told of him that when he permitted the out-going choristers to come into the organ-loft, he was wont frequently to say while he was playing: "Come, come, don't stand there idle, but give us a hand on the key-board," a request as stupid as it was impracticable. He was only eighteen when he was appointed, in 1752, as conductor of the Ancient Academy of Music. Five years later, when Bernard Gates made up his mind to retire to Church Aston in Oxfordshire, Cooke was appointed master of the choristers at the Abbey, and a year later he was made a lay-vicar. When his master, John Robinson, for whom he had acted as deputy, died in 1762, he became organist at the Abbey. He held this situation thirteen years, and then was seized with an ambition to attain academical distinction. He graduated by accumulation Doctor of Music at Cambridge in 1775, and in seven years afterwards was admitted *ad eundem gradem* at Oxford. In 1782 he became organist of St. Martin's in the Fields, and in 1789 he resigned the conductorship of the Ancient Academy of Music to Dr. Arnold. Cooke was an industrious collector of music, compiled a number of compositions of all sorts by writers of all nations and ages, and copied and scored them with his own hand. A collection of nineteen volumes, including many of his own compositions, now in the library of the Sacred Harmonic Society, testifies to his industry and cosmopolitan taste. Many of the pieces contained in this collection have not been published. His own works comprise many anthems, services, glees, odes, cantatas, chants, psalm and hymn tunes. He wrote only one piece for the theatre, an ode for the tragedy of *The Captives*. His Church music is chiefly represented in the present day by the bright and effective service in G, none of his anthems having been reprinted in modern times. These, as far as can be judged from the silent copies, are not wanting in either science, expression, or dignity. Many of his glees are very popular with those who know how to appreciate in a proper fashion this half-forgotten delight. When the day returns which shall find men longing for sweet melodies treated with sufficient science to give a zest to their enjoyment, Cooke's glees will again become favourites.

Another Church musician who also wrote glees and secular music, and "gained a good and lasting fame thereby," was Jonathan Battishill. In the notice of the life and labours of Matthew Lock, it was shown that he began by writing Church music, and preferred in his later time to build his fame on his productions for secular occasions—a course of proceeding not uninfluenced by the treatment which his first published attempt received at the hands of his brethren of the Chapel Royal. In the case of Battishill, the conditions were in some sort reversed. He made his fame as a writer for the stage, and only turned his attention to sacred music in his later days, when his feelings were softened by affliction. It may be that his mind reverted to the days of his childhood, the many happy hours he had spent as a chorister in St. Paul's, and he sought to change the current of his ideas in music by devoting some time to Church composition. He wrote several anthems, some of which were published in Page's *Harmonia Sacra*, or separately as *Six Anthems and Ten Chants*, the first in 1800, the second in 1804. Of these anthems, "Call to remembrance" is one of the most beautiful, devotional, and expressive compositions, and will live as long as men can appreciate the value of the tender sentiment of graceful melodies, interwoven with ingenious counterpoint. "Behold how good" and "O Lord, look down" are for five voices, "I will magnify Thee" for six, and "Call to remembrance" for seven. All these exhibit much ability in contrivance, and prove that a long course of practice in the production of light and trivial gems had not deadened his knowledge, or rendered him unskilful in the manipulation of the graver scientific uses of musical art.

Jonathan Battishill, the son of a solicitor, Jonathan Battishill, and the grandson of the Rev. Jonathan Battishill of Sheepwash, in Devonshire, was born in London in 1738. At the age of nine he was admitted to the choir of St. Paul's under William Savage, then Almoner, to whom he became articled when he left the choir. In 1757 Battishill wrote songs for Sadlers Wells Theatre, and in the year following began to act as deputy for Dr. Boyce at the Chapel Royal. He was engaged shortly after at Covent Garden Theatre as conductor, as the harpsichord player was then called, and here he met Miss Davies, the original performer of Madge in *Love in a Village*, whom he married in 1763. In 1764 his *Almena* was produced, but failed in consequence of the poverty of the libretto. "Some of the choruses in *Almena*, for science, dignity, and expression, deserve to be classed with the first-rate productions." He wrote many songs for Samuel Champness, at that time a favourite concert and theatre vocalist, and a deputy at St. Paul's, who had a fine bass voice. "Most of his songs are extremely energetic and vigorous; this in particular is the characteristic of the two bass songs, 'Pois'd in heaven's eternal scale,' and 'Thus when young Ammon march'd along,' which were written for Champness. As proofs of the beauty and originality of his fancy in ballad compositions, every one will admit the charming pastoral melody of 'Ye Shepherds and Nymphs of the Grove;' the mellifluous and affecting air of 'When Damon languished at my feet;' the expressive passages in 'When beauty on the lover's cheek;' and, above all, his popular song of 'Kate of Aberdeen.'"

Battishill wrote several glees, for one of which, "Underneath the Myrtle Shade," he was awarded the prize given by the Noblemen's Catch Club in 1770; for another, "Come bind my hair," he gained a prize in 1771. In 1776 he published by subscription two collections of three and four part songs. At this time he was organist at Christ Church, Newgate Street, holding a like place at St. Clement's, Eastcheap. He was considered the most extraordinary extempore player of his time, and a most accomplished organist. His memory was prodigious; he not only could play a piece which he had carefully read through once, but could at any time afterwards recall it with a slight effort of memory. He once played to Dr. Arnold the greater part of his oratorio, *The Prodigal Son*, which the author had nearly forgotten. The most singular part of the story is that Battishill had never seen a copy of the work, and had only heard it twice some thirty years previously. In the year 1775 his wife, who had retired from the stage on her marriage, and with whom he had lived in love and harmony for twelve years, died, and several stories are told of the effect which her death had upon his mind and habits. One rumour relates that "from this period he dissipated much of his time in convivial parties, and so far gave way to excess as gradually to undermine his constitution." As he lived for more than a quarter of a century after the death of his wife, a second story is more likely to be true, namely, "that her death so affected him that he desisted from composition, and devoted much time to his books, of which he had collected between six and seven thousand volumes, chiefly classical works." It is not possible to credit the tradition that he wrote the anthem, "Call to remembrance," in the billiard-room of the Queen's Head Tavern in Newgate Street, in an agony of remorse after a bout of dissipation. The ingenuity and thought involved in the construction of the anthem stands as proof to the contrary. His last days were spent in peaceful retirement, "the anxious spirit of research" which one of his biographers states to have moved his mind in his early youth not having deserted him in his old age. He died December 10th, 1801, in his sixty-third year, and was buried in St. Paul's Cathedral, near to Dr. Boyce, whom he served faithfully, and whose works and character he always admired.

CHAPTER XIII.

SAMUEL ARNOLD, JOHN STAFFORD SMITH, JOHN CHRISTMAS
BECKWITH, WILLIAM CHARD, THOMAS ATTWOOD, JOHN
CLARKE WHITFIELD, WILLIAM CROTCH.

MEDIOCRITY in Church music was triumphant at the
latter part of the eighteenth century. The best music
in use for the services of the Church was that which
was supplied from the stores of the past. The composers of the then present who had the power to
command an introduction for their works, exhibited in
them a large acquaintance with the music of Handel,
and excellent memories which supplied the place of
invention. The interest in English musical art seems
to have decayed, and although music was patronised by
royalty and the nobility, the programmes most attractive
for the public were those formed from the works of foreign
writers. When English music was permitted a hearing,
it was upon sufferance, and English musicians writing,
whether for the stage, the concert-room, or the Church,
were constrained to mould their designs after foreign
patterns. Church music was not encouraged, and
musicians, then as now, worked in the fields that paid
best, not always mindful of the mute appeals of an art
which neglect had crippled. The attempts made to re-
vive an interest in ecclesiastical music for the Anglican
Church service resulted in failure. Dr. Boyce, when he
published his *Cathedral Music*, "had to complain of
want of patronage;" his successor, Dr. Arnold, met with

a like ill-result, though not without some foreboding
of the matter. In 1790 his four volumes of *Cathedral
Music*, "being a collection in score of the most valuable
and useful compositions for Cathedral use by the several
English masters of the seventeenth and eighteenth
centuries," were dedicated to George III., and the preface, dated from 480, Strand, November 1st, reveals the
estimation in which the compiler held his art, his latent
suspicions of unrequited labour, and the state of the
popular mind with regard to Church music.

The work, which cost much time, labour, and money,
was very indifferently supported, about 120 copies only
were subscribed for. This does not lessen the value of
the effort made by Dr. Arnold, neither does it show that
he was indifferent to the merits of that department of
music with which from his earliest years he had been
familiar.

Samuel Arnold was born on August 10th, 1740, and
became a chorister in the Chapel Royal under Bernard
Gates and Dr. Nares. He was engaged before he had
attained his twenty-third year as composer to Covent
Garden Theatre, where he brought out *The Maid of
the Mill*, a *pasticcio*, in which Mr. Jonathan Battishill
presided at the harpsichord in the orchestra. In this
opera the first attempt was made since the days of Purcell,
with very great success, to introduce choruses as part of
the action. He produced the music for forty-three operas,
after-pieces, and pantomimes, between the years 1765
and 1802, many of which contain melodies "which the
world will not willingly let die."

In sacred music he was equally adventurous. He

wrote an oratorio in 1767, *The Cure of Saul*, in 1768, and two following years he produced *Abimelech*, *The Resurrection*, and *The Prodigal Son*, which last named work was performed at Oxford when Lord North was made Chancellor in 1773. In 1769 he purchased Marylebone Gardens, but lost much money in the attempt to carry on the entertainments on a superior scale. On the occasion of the installation of Lord North alluded to, Arnold was offered an honorary degree in music, which he declined, preferring to present himself for examination in the customary way. Dr. Hayes, the Professor, returned his exercise unopened with the reply, "Sir, it is quite unnecessary to scrutinise an exercise written by the composer of *The Prodigal Son*."

Soon after his appointment as organist and composer to the Chapel Royal in succession to Dr. Nares in 1783, he began to collect the materials for his *Cathedral Music*, in four volumes.

In conjunction with Dr. Callcott he published a work called, *The Psalms of David; for the Use of Parish Churches. The Words selected by the Rev. Sir Adam Gordon, Bart., M.A., London*, 1791. In friendly partnership with Callcott he also established the Glee Club. He was at this time carrying on the publication of a splendid edition of the works of Handel, which he had commenced in 1786. He extended the work to 168 numbers, making about thirty-six volumes, but was unable to complete his design for want of patronage. He found time to attend to other duties, and accepted the post of conductor of the Academy of Ancient

Music. At the death of Dr. Cooke he was appointed organist of Westminster Abbey, and after the decease of Hayes became conductor of the Festival of the Sons of the Clergy in St. Paul's, Mr. Attwood, then newly appointed, presiding at the organ. He died on October 22nd, 1802, his death being hastened probably by a fall from his library steps. After his death, in 1810, an oratorio of his composition, *Elijah*, was produced, but without success. He wrote several services, and nearly forty anthems, but his labours in each case are represented to posterity by single works. The first class by his evening Service in A, in continuation of Boyce's Morning Service, and the second by his anthem, "Who is this?" printed in Page's *Harmonia Sacra*. A treatise on Thorough Bass which he had written with a view to the suggestion of new readings of old rules, was never published. His son was a dramatic author, and for a long time was the lessee of the English Opera-house, now the Lyceum Theatre, where many most interesting works were produced under his direction.

Almost equally industrious, or at all events prolific, in the production of Services and Anthems was John Stafford Smith, but he is even less known to posterity for his Church works than his friend Dr. Arnold. Out of a list of about thirty anthems of various degrees of length and value, not one has been reprinted since the original issue in 1793. For every musician who knows and loves his glees, for every musical historian who has read and studied his *Musica Antiqua*, there are hundreds who have never heard that he wrote any anthems "for the choir service of the Church of England." This is not because they are deficient in merit—the composer of "While fools their time," "Blest pair of Syrens," "Return, blest days," "When to the Muses' Haunted Hill," and other glees, could not have been an indifferent musician—but because his work was born out of its time. John Stafford Smith's name will be remembered for his glees; his fame may also rest upon the fact that he was the instructor of John Goss. Smith was born at Gloucester in 1750, his father being at that time organist of the cathedral. After some preliminary instruction at home he was admitted into the Chapel Royal under Boyce. He began to write glees while he was yet young, and in 1771 competed for the prizes given by the Catch Club. He was afterwards one of the lay-vicars at Westminster Abbey, and was appointed Master of the Children of the Chapel Royal in 1802. In addition to the anthems, he published *A Collection of English Songs, in score for three and four voices, composed about the year 1500. Taken from MSS. of the same age, London, 1779 ;* and *Musica Antiqua, a selection of music of this and other countries from the commencement of the twelfth to the beginning of the eighteenth century, comprising some of the earliest and most curious motetts, madrigals, hymns, anthems, songs, lessons, and dance tunes ; some of them now first published from manuscripts and printed works of great rarity and value. The whole calculated to show the original sources of the melody and harmony of this country, and to exhibit the different styles and degrees of improvement of the several periods, London,* 1812. This work is often referred to, but few who have not seen the book itself can divine the nature and value of its contents. Smith died in 1836, in the eighty-sixth year of his age.

The anthems of John Christmas Beckwith achieved better success than attended those of Stafford Smith. Many of them are still popular, and retain a good position, even though the tide of popular estimation has set against them. Such anthems as " The Lord is very great " and "My soul is weary " are dramatic in form, and aim at something higher than that which was attained by the composers of the latter decade of the last century. They represent, however, the simple wild flowers of musical eloquence, which were to become the garden-blooms of a later time. In them may be seen the proposals of a design, very much favoured by subsequent composers, namely, the development of the organ part into a sort of obbligato solo, which seems to have been a device originated by Beckwith. The earlier composers confined their organ speech to simple accompaniments, at first identical with the voices as exemplified in Greene, Hayes, and Nares, afterwards by the introduction of *ritornelli;* while Beckwith gave the organ independent counterpoint. His suggestion was eagerly seized by later writers, and though this novel use of the organ aroused many opponents at the outset, it gradually found supporters, then admirers, and then imitators, and Church music entered upon a new phase of life.

Beckwith was also noteworthy as a thoughtful musioian in other respects. He published a set of chants with the title, *The First Verse of every Psalm of David, with an ancient or modern chant, in score, adapted as much as possible to the sentiment of each Psalm,* **1808.**   In this work he proposed to encourage congregational singing by a system of marking the places of the emphasis in chanting in the Prayer Books.   This was the first suggestion of the marked Psalter.   Before that time chanting was chiefly confined to cathedrals, and each choir had its own tradition, more or less good or bad according to the state of discipline observed.   For these reasons the name of John Christmas Beckwith deserves honourable place in a list of English Church composers.   Like Birde, Gibbons, and Purcell, Beckwith came of a musical stock.   His uncle, nephews, brothers, and other relations distinguished themselves after their manner, but John Christmas was the genius of the family.   He was so called because he was born on Christmas Day, 1759. He was a pupil of Dr. Philip Hayes, and became organist of the church of St. Peter, Mancroft, in Norwich, in 1780.   He graduated at Oxford, by accumulation, Mus. Bac. and Mus. Doc. on July 5th, 1803, and died on June 3rd, 1809.   He was an excellent teacher of singing; the celebrated Thomas Vaughan was one of his pupils, and Dr. Buck, afterwards organist of Norwich Cathedral, who studied under him, acquired from him that power of training choristers for which he was so famous.   Beckwith was also an accomplished draughtsman and painter, as well as a good and earnest musician.

In the records of cathedral music the name of William Chard may have a place, inasmuch as he was in his day famous for training boys' voices, and obtained a reputation as the composer of pretty anthems. Of these he wrote a large number, none of which satisfy modern requirements, though they were very popular at one time. He was born about 1765, was a chorister at St. Paul's under Robert Hudson, Mus. Bac. He was appointed as a singing-man at Winchester Cathedral in 1787, and afterwards organist there and at the college. He graduated at Oxford in 1812, and died May 23rd, 1849, in the eighty-fourth year of his age. Some of his anthems, as well as some glees by him, have been printed.

The music of the Church, notwithstanding earnest efforts of single enthusiasts to uphold its character, was now suffering a change. There were few original writers, and the old style of composition, instead of being allowed to develop in its natural course, was torn up by the roots, and exotic plants inserted in its place. The day had not arrived when men would complacently listen to anthems which were adaptations of music composed for other rituals. Public opinion revolted at the idea of anything that was called papistical, a name applied to any music that had been first written to adorn the service of the Roman Catholic Church. Even Handel was only admitted through the mutilations of Pitt, as Mozart was through those of Pratt. Anything that was pretty and florid, however weak and vapid, if it was composed expressly for the service of the Anglican Church, was accepted as a pious offering without question as to its value. It was thus that the music of the Church was at a very low ebb at the end of the last century, when Thomas Attwood became organist of St. Paul's. The old writers were neglected, and nothing that was then new was good. Posterity therefore revenges itself upon its indifferent progenitors by neglecting all that seemed to give their trivial minds delight. Attwood set a good example by approaching the duties he felt called upon to perform, with an earnestness of purpose and piety of intention that could not fail to be effective in course of time, if not at once.

Thomas Attwood was born in 1767, in London, where his father was a coal-merchant, and a musician— a player upon the viola and the trumpet. He was admitted to the Chapel Royal in 1776, and as one of "Dr. Nares's boys," learned to sing sweetly, and comport himself so as to gain the esteem of all. In the latter part of the time during which he was in the Chapel he had the advantage of studying under Dr. Ayrton. When he was sixteen his voice broke, and his behaviour and abilities recommended him to the notice of the Prince of Wales, afterwards George IV. There being no suitable academy in England, he was sent to Italy to pursue his musical studies. Attwood selected Naples to begin with, and remained there two years under Filippo Cinque and Gaetano Latilla. He next visited Vienna, where he became the pupil of Mozart, who acknowledged in after time that Attwood had imbibed more of his own style than any other of his pupils. The amiability of the two musicians made them well suited to each other, and they became firm friends. On Attwood's return to England, in 1787, he was appointed organist of the church of St. George the Martyr, Queen Square. His royal patron continued to exercise an interest in his welfare, and in 1791 he was named musical instructor to the Duchess of York, and afterwards to the Princess of Wales. In 1796 he became organist of St. Paul's, and composer to the Chapel Royal, in succession to John Jones at the first place, and to Dr. Dupuis at the second. He was appointed organist to the Chapel Royal at Brighton in 1821, and in 1836, on the death of John Stafford Smith, became organist of the Chapel Royal, St. James's. For a period of a quarter of a century, that is to say from the years 1791 to 1816, Attwood wrote many works for stage representation. The merits of his music no one called into question, but it is asserted "that he never made any very great success."

It will be seen that Attwood continued to write for the stage long after the date of his appointment to St. Paul's, but subsequently discontinued it, whether discouraged by the circumstances of ill-success or for other reasons, it is not necessary for the present purpose to inquire. Though still invited by managers to write, he gave the work into other hands. One libretto received from Mr. Arnold he intrusted to a clever pupil of his, John Goss, who made therewith his first and only essay at theatrical composition.

It has been affirmed that Attwood wrote anthems for the use of the Chapel Royal and St. Paul's soon after his appointment. There are no copies of such music in the books of St. Paul's other than the music for the funeral of Lord Nelson in 1805, and the parts of the Service in D. There are also no copies of his music in the books of the Chapel Royal. In those days the authorities refused to incur the expense of transcribing, so that the composer had to have the copies made at his own cost when his music was done. Most of Attwood's sacred music was printed after his death in 1853, under the editorship of his god-son, Thomas Attwood Walmisley. The beautiful little anthems, " Turn thy face," and " Come Holy Ghost," were written for insertion in a musical magazine ; and of his very fine anthems with orchestral accompaniments, " I was glad," and " O Lord, grant the king,"—the one was composed for the coronation of George IV., and the other for William IV. He had undertaken a third for the coronation of Queen Victoria, but he did not live to complete it. His pupil, and successor at the organ at St. Paul's, John Goss, at the suggestion of the Duke of Wellington, composed an anthem for the occasion, which had for the title, " O Lord, grant the king," and contained a very beautiful treble solo. It was printed, but was only once performed at St. Paul's.

Attwood wrote a large number of sonatas, songs, and glees. Among the songs may be mentioned, " The Soldier's Dream," and among the glees, " In peace love tunes the shepherd's reed," and " The Curfew," still well remembered and often sung.

When Mendelssohn first visited London he stayed at the house of Attwood at Norwood, and there are several allusions to these visits in his letters. There is also a composition extant, in which Mendelssohn introduces the tone of Attwood's gate-bell, which used to sound the signal for departure. By the invitation of Attwood, Mendelssohn very frequently played upon the St. Paul's organ, and the three preludes and fugues which he wrote for the instrument are dedicated to Attwood.

Attwood was one of the founders of the Philharmonic Society, and on more than one occasion conducted the concerts. Personally he was regarded as an amiable and just man, of refined tastes and pursuits. His anthems prove him to have been possessed of the power of writing expressively and with a certain amount of tenderness of phrasing and emphasis.

In his later years Attwood lived in Cheyne Walk in Chelsea, and there he died on March 28th, 1838, in the seventy-first year of his age.

Thirty years ago no music was more generally popular than Attwood's services and Clarke-Whitfield's anthems. The former have grown out of use in consequence of an objection to the general use of the *Jubilate*, the *Cantate Domino* and the *Deus misereatur* which has sprung up; and the latter have disappeared from the service lists because they are old fashioned and are said inadequately to represent the dignity of worship.

John Clarke was born at Gloucester, December 13th, 1770, was a chorister of St. John's College, Oxford, and received his musical education under Dr. Philip Hayes. In his nineteenth year he was appointed organist at the church of St. Lawrence, Ludlow; occupying himself there both in teaching and in reading for his Bachelor's degree in music, which he took at Oxford in 1793. Two years later he was organist at Armagh Cathedral, a place which, however, he held but a short time; for in 1795 he was organist and master of the choristers at the cathedrals of St. Patrick and Christ Church, Dublin. When the rebellion of 1798 broke out, he left Ireland and returned to England, where he applied for and obtained the position of organist and master of the choristers to St. John's and Trinity Colleges, in Cambridge. Here he took his Doctor's degree, and was admitted in 1810 *ad eundem gradem* at Oxford. He left Cambridge and went to Hereford, and had scarcely been there a year when, upon the death of Dr. Hague, he obtained the office of Professor of Music in the University of Cambridge. He still held his appointment at Hereford, but resigned it in 1833, in consequence of an attack of paralysis, and was succeeded by Samuel Sebastian Wesley. He died near Hereford on February 22nd, 1836, and was buried in the cloisters of the cathedral there. He assumed the name of Whitfield in addition to his own upon the occasion of his inheriting some property from an uncle in 1814. His activity and industry were only equalled by his restlessness. He wrote Several services in different keys —in E, E flat, F, C, A minor, and D, together with many anthems, some of which have been printed, while others are not published.

He also edited a collection of thirty anthems by other musicians, and composed an oratorio, *The Crucifixion and the Resurrection*, produced at the Hereford Festival of 1822. Clarke-Whitfield further wrote a number of songs, glees, and some instrumental pieces, and edited an edition of some of Handel's works, for which he made a pianoforte score, the first time the attempt had been made, previous editions having only a figured bass.

The last noteworthy composer of Church music born within the limit of the last century, was William Crotch. He was not, however, so highly eminent as a Church composer as he was as a teacher. He displayed a certain amount of ability throughout his life, as a player, as a lecturer, and as a composer, but it cannot be said with any truth that be fully realised the hopes formed of his talents in early childhood. He was born at Norwich, July 5th, 1770. His father was a carpenter and had built himself an organ, whereon he was wont to amuse himself in his leisure hours. His little son when not more than two years old contrived to get to the organ and to play a tune which his fond father conceived to be remarkably like " God save the King." After a few trials the child managed to add a bass, and soon his little repertory was increased by the addition of other tunes. His ear was remarkably sensitive, and as soon as he knew how to express himself was able to name any note that he heard struck. The Hon. Daines Barrington gave an account of the child, and Dr. Burney wrote a description of the powers of this young phenomenon in the *Philosophical Transactions* of 1779. In the year following, before he was ten years old, he played in public in London. · When he was fourteen he composed an oratorio, *The Captivity of Judah*, which was performed in 1789 at Cambridge, in which place he went to reside three years previously. He was assistant to Dr. Randall, at that time organist to King's and Trinity Colleges, and the Professor of Music in the University.

After having remained **Dr.** Randall's deputy for two years he left for Oxford, with the intention of studying for the Church, but his patron, the Rev. A. Schonberg, dying, he applied for the post of organist at Christ Church, Oxford, and entered upon his duties there in 1791. Four years later he graduated as Mus. Bac.; and on the death of Dr. Philip Hayes, in 1797, was made organist of St. John's and Professor of Music at Oxford. When two more years had passed he became Doctor of Music (Nov. 21st, 1799), his exercise being a setting of Warton's "Ode to Fancy," which he afterwards printed. His oratorio *Palestine*, the words by Bishop Heber, was produced at the Hanover Square Rooms in 1812. In the same year his *Elements of Musical Composition* was published. He had already since his appointment at Oxford as Professor distinguished himself by the character of his lectures; an opportunity for addressing a wider area soon now presented itself, when he was appointed in 1820 as Lecturer to the Royal Institution. Two years later, when the Royal Academy was founded, Crotch was named as the first Principal, continuing in that office until his death. He wrote an oratorio, the *Captivity of Judah*, an entirely different work to his former effort with the same title, for the installation of the Duke of Wellington as Chancellor of the University of Oxford in 1834. After a life of usefulness he died suddenly at the house of his son, Head Master of the Grammar School at Taunton, on December 29th, 1847, and was buried at Bishop's Hull, a short distance from Taunton. He composed several glees, some fugues and pieces for the organ; an ode on the accession of George

IV., 1820; funeral anthem on the death of the Duke of
York in 1829; "The Lord is King," anthem for voices
and orchestra, 1843, performed once or twice by the
Sacred Harmonic Society in times past; a motett, "Me-
thinks I hear the full Celestial Choir;" and ten anthems
in score. There are three volumes of *Specimens of
various Styles of Music referred to in a course of Lectures
read in Oxford and London,* of his compilation. The
substance of many of these lectures he also printed, as
well as a work on *Thorough Bass and Harmony.* One of
his pieces frequently sung as an anthem, "Lo, Star-led
Chiefs," is from his oratorio *Palestine.* His Church
music is always pleasing, though it cannot be said to
express dignity in a high form. It is written with all
the power of one familiar with scientific resource; the
melodies are often very beautiful, and the harmonies
striking. But there is not often a feeling of exaltation
brought to the mind by his music as a whole, though
in parts there are touches of masterly artistic power.
One of his anthems, "Sing we merrily," has a beautiful
verse, "Take the Psalm," but the melody to the opening
words, and the organ introduction, are so like the air of
a well-known comic song that the anthem is commonly
known by the irreverent title of the "Billy Taylor"
anthem. Dr. Crotch was as facilé with the artist's
pencil as with the music pen, and many of his drawings
are beautiful and valuable as well for their own merit
as for the skill with which the several scenes are
depicted. He possessed humour and the power of ex-
pressing humorous scenes with much force. He more
than once acted as one of the judges appointed to

examine the compositions sent in for the prize given by Miss Hackett, and known as the "Gresham prize." On one occasion Alfred Angel obtained the medal for his anthem, "Blow ye the trumpet in Zion," his fellow competitor being Samuel Sebastian Wesley, with his immortal anthem, "The Wilderness." Crotch objected to the novel form of the whole design, and expressed his opinion of the work in very characteristic fashion by drawing the portrait of a chorister boy with his face distorted with agony in the effort to reach the high A in the concluding verse, "And sorrow and sighing." Posterity has, in this instance, reversed the judgment of the expert.

CHAPTER XIV.

WILLIAM RICHARD BEXFIELD, WILLIAM STERNDALE BENNETT, THOMAS ATTWOOD WALMISLEY, SAMUEL SEBASTIAN WESLEY, HENRY SMART, JOHN GOSS.

THE English Church composers born within the first quarter of the present century proved themselves to be possessed of a different degree of thought with regard to their views as to the mission of Church music. By the time most of these had reached the full tide of life, and the very youngest had attained the age when they might be influenced by outside events, all were subjected to the rise of a fresh tide of thought in Church matters, including a revival of Church art, literature, and music. Those who were most enthusiastic as leaders in the matter found, on reviewing the music for the sanctuary, much that was, if not actually corrupt, quite unfit for association with the vigorous new life that was born. The need was urgent, the supply to meet the taste was non-existent. A return to that which had been in old time was deemed politic and proper. Societies were formed for the purpose of reviving the archaic in music, and what was called the Gregorian movement was instituted. The tones or melodies were assumed to have been associated with all that was sacred and memorable in the history of religion and the Church. Men believed what they desired to believe, and accepted without questioning that which ministered to their wants aroused by the prevalent fancy. Meanwhile Church composers worked steadily and earnestly, without being in the slightest degree influenced by the mediævalism which threatened to envelop all Church music in a veil of darkness and barbarity. The adherents of this system applied the necessary counterbalance to a form of hymn-tunes which had sprung up of luscious melody and fascinating rhythm. Composers for the Church, believing rather in their own already formed views of the mission they had to fulfil, namely, to aid the advance, not the retrogression, of musical art, suffered themselves to be little influenced by this movement other than by the occasional tonal expression tenderly introduced. They believed that the real life of Church composition began with the old fathers of the sixteenth century, and not with any accommodated forms of

melodies of marked character, and doubtful antiquity.
Not one of the composers whose names head this
chapter betray in their works any marked influence
which this class-music exercised over their thoughts.
They were unquestionably aware of the movement
made by one section of the rulers in the Church, but
they apparently sought to carry on the tradition set
by their predecessors as English Church composers, and
to do the best in their power not to follow a faction,
but to write for the general good.

It is sad to think that the list of names of writers
honourable for their deeds in these latter years is a
small one. It is an honourable one. It is also not
a little singular that the owners of the names, born in
the succession in which their names stand, should
have ended their earthly pilgrimage almost in the
inverse proportion to their birth. The last-named,
William Richard Bexfield, died the first, having only
attained his twenty-seventh year. He was born at
Norwich on April 27th, 1824, and in 1832 became a
chorister under Dr. Buck, when he became remarkable
for the sweetness of his voice and the charm of his
singing. When he left the choir he applied himself
to the study of music almost without a master to help
and guide him, yet he made rapid progress in playing
and composition. His first organ appointment was at
Boston, in Lincolnshire. Here he remained about four
or five years, when he left to become organist at St.
Helen's, Bishopsgate, the parish fraught with so many
musical recollections of the reign of Elizabeth—where
Birde, Wilbye, and Sir Thomas Gresham lived. In

London Bexfield had the opportunity of becoming acquainted with all that was being done in the world of music, while he continued to work earnestly and conscientiously.   In 1849 he graduated Doctor of Music at Cambridge, having previously taken the degree of Bachelor at Oxford in 1846. He wrote an oratorio, *Israel Restored*, which was performed on September 22, 1852, at Norwich, his native city, during one of the customary festivals, and awakened much interest.   When the same work was given at the Albert Hall a short time back, the public had forgotten all about the author, and had in the meantime modified its opinions with regard to what was pleasing in the construction of sacred music. He died, October 29, 1853, and the promise of excellence his work offered was cut off. He published a set of fugues for the organ, which were greatly admired, and some Church anthems in score, to which his portrait is prefixed.

The name of William Sterndale Bennett properly belongs to another department in music, and his life and labours demand to be set forth in greater detail than would be allowed or might be expected here. Notwithstanding the circumstances which surrounded his after-career, he seems never to have been unmindful of the claims of the school in which he received his early education; and although his contributions to Church music are not numerous, they are of sufficient character to be representative, and to justify a short record of his life and the insertion of his name in a list of English Church composers. Like Purcell, he came of a musical family. He was born at Sheffield, April 13th, 1816.

In 1824 he was admitted as a chorister in the Chapel of King's College, in Cambridge; and entered as a student of the Royal Academy in London when he was only ten years of age. His compositions, even in his early youth, were original and individual, as in fact they remained throughout his life, for all that opinions are divided on the subject. His friendship with Mendelssohn and Schumann, formed whilst he was studying in Leipzig, rather helped him to strive to preserve his own individuality in composition than induced him to imitate that which he held in admiration.

There are only four or five of his anthems known; these are constructed in a manner entirely different to the ordinary fashion, and for this reason may be mentioned as marking a particular desire on the part of the composer to bring the resources of modern use to bear on this form of composition, and thus to leave to posterity the impress of the modifications of thought born in the present age.

Those which have been printed are " O that I knew," for St. Thomas's Day, " Remember now thy Creator," " The fool hath said in his heart," and " Now my God, let, I beseech Thee." There is also an adaptation by Dr. Steggall of two numbers from the *Woman of Samaria* —" God is a spirit " and " Blessed be the Lord God," woven into one to form an anthem ; and a portion of an unpublished motett, " In thee, O Lord," which has been performed by the Bach Choir. The *Chorale Book*, edited in conjunction with Otto Goldschmidt, may be also included in the list of his contributions to Church music.

His labours in the cause of music and his eminence in the art received some recognition in his own time. He was elected by a large majority to fill the chair of Music in the University of Cambridge in 1856, and received the degree of Doctor in Music. A year after that he was admitted to the degree of honorary M.A., and, at the same time, the small stipend of the professor was augmented by an additional annual payment of £100. In 1858 his *May Queen* was produced at Leeds, and his *Woman of Samaria* at Birmingham in 1867. In 1870 he received the honorary degree of D.C.L. from the University of Oxford, on the recommendation of his brother professor, Sir Frederick A. Gore Ouseley, Bart.; and in 1871 the Queen conferred upon him the honour of knighthood, the first distinction of the kind which any English Church composer had received. In 1872 a scholarship in his name was founded at the Royal Academy of Music, of which establishment he had been principal since 1866, and the scholarship was presented to him as a public testimonial. He died February 1st, 1875, and received a public funeral in Westminster Abbey five days afterwards. He lies by the side of Henry Purcell.

The Cambridge professor whom Sterndale Bennett succeeded was Thomas Attwood Walmisley, a musician who did much, and perhaps might have done much more, for the exaltation of his profession, had he lived in times more favourable for the cultivation of art. He was the son of Thomas Forbes Walmisley, organist of St. Martin's in the Fields, London, a musician of merit, and the godson of Thomas Attwood, after whom he was named. He was born January 21st, 1814. In his young days he gave signs of much musical appreciation, and received lessons from his father and godfather. He went to Cambridge as organist of Trinity and St. John's Colleges and matriculated in 1832, and was admitted M.A. in 1837, a year after he had been appointed Professor of Music in the University in succession to Dr. Clarke-Whitfield. He did not, however, take the degree of Mus. Doc. until 1847. He was highly esteemed as an organ-player, and as a composer he was full of fancy; some of his songs, trios, and glees, are remarkable for the grace of the treatment and the originality of the themes. There is unquestionable force and spirit in his ideas, but there is also not an absence of discipline so much as a disregard of it in more than one of his compositions. That he was capable of giving form and shape to his ideas of "jubilant religious music, which shows the singer prayerful yet joyous," may be seen in the little gem of an anthem, "Not unto us," which is a great favourite in choirs. To an over-sensitive mind, such as he possessed, the desire to be free from the burning current of his own thoughts which led he knew not whither, suggested an unwise indulgence in lethal remedies. His pleasures may have been thus augmented but his life was shortened, and he died comparatively a young man on January 17th, 1856, in the forty-second year of his age. His father, who survived him, published in 1857 a collection of his compositions for the Church, all of which are in constant use in one or other of the cathedrals and churches of the Anglican communion.

The two greatest names of this epoch in Church music are unquestionably those of Wesley and Goss. They were Church musicians who made offering of the purest style of devotional music, the inheritance of a long line of illustrious predecessors, with such additions as would come from the right use of modern knowledge.

Samuel Sebastian Wesley, named after his father and his father's idol, John Sebastian Bach, was born in London in 1810. His father was well known as one of the most able organists of his day, a musician who, as a child, showed as much genius as young Crotch, and in later years strove by precept and example to impress his countrymen with a love for the works of the great Leipzig Cantor. Many other of Wesley's relatives have become famous for their musical powers through a long line of descent, and it may be interesting to state that the family is derived from the same stock from which came Garrat Wellesley, Earl of Mornington, and the father of the Duke of Wellington, and Sir Frederick Arthur Gore Ouseley, the present Professor of Music in Oxford.

The subject of the present notice was admitted at the age of six into Christ's Hospital; this place he left in 1819 to become a chorister of the Chapel Royal, where he remained eight years under Mr. Hawes and Mr. Molineux. He was one of the two children selected by Attwood to assist in the service at the Chapel Royal, Brighton, established by George IV., then recently come to the throne. When he had scarcely attained the age of seventeen he was appointed organist to St. James's Church in the Hampstead Road; in 1829 he obtained a like post at St. Giles's, Camberwell, where he formed acquaintance with Thomas Adams, then noted as the best extempore organist of the day, who was at the new church, St. George's, in the same parish. Young Wesley's budding genius was expanded by the good counsel and advice of the more experienced player, and from him he was encouraged to persevere until in his turn he gained a reputation as an extempore player of high merit. In 1829 he also accepted the place of organist at St. John's, Waterloo Road. He did not seem to be afraid of any amount of work, and undertook as many tasks as would have daunted one less courageous. In 1830 he engaged to play at the parish church at Hampton at the evening service of Sunday— being probably tempted thereto by the prospect of indulging in an occasional piscatorial ramble—for which purpose he drove post after the morning service at Camberwell. Such an amount of work naturally in course of time excited a longing for quietness and rest. This seemed to offer itself when, in 1833, Dr. Clarke-Whitfield resigned the post of organist at Hereford in consequence of failing health. Wesley was gladly welcomed to his new home. He had the repose and recognition he longed for, the rest he hoped earnestly to enjoy. The Wye also was a good fishing river. The society of the Close was congenial to his refined and sensitive disposition. Here he found also the means of cultivating the domestic virtues, for in 1835 he married the sister of Dean Mereweather. His first anthem,

"Blessed be the God and Father," was written during his stay at Hereford for an Easter Sunday service at which only the boys and one efficient male voice was available. He also assisted at the triennial festivals, at Worcester first as pianist in 1833, and at Hereford as conductor, by the usual right of the organist, in 1834. Upon this occasion his father's "Exultate Deo," and some sacred pieces and an overture of his own composition were given. In the following year at Gloucester he produced a new quartett, "Millions of spiritual creatures." At the end of 1835 he migrated to Exeter and continued there for nearly seven years. Some time before he had sent his anthem, "The Wilderness," to compete for the Gresham prize, the result of which has been related in the notice of the life of Dr. Crotch (p. 160). In 1841 he took the degree of Doctor of Music at Oxford, by accumulation, for the purpose of giving himself an extra qualification as a candidate for the post of Professor of Music in the University of Edinburgh, at that time vacant through the death of John Thomson. He was not successful, but still he went north, and became organist of the parish church at Leeds. Here he found a choir worthy of the best efforts of his genius.

In 1849 he removed to Winchester for the purpose of obtaining the advantages of the college for the education of his sons, and there he resided for fifteen years; adding very little to the stores of Cathedral music by his compositions, and disheartened and discouraged by the want of patronage for all efforts of the sort, whether by himself or others. On May 24th, 1849, he published a pamphlet, couched in a suggestive rather than in a practical spirit, entitled, *A Few Words on Cathedral Music, and the Musical System of the National Church, with a Plan of Reform.* At the end of the pamphlet he quoted two magnificent motetts, written by his father, "*Tu es Sacerdos*" for six voices, and "*Omnia Vanitas*" for five, as "a proof that talent of the highest order of ecclesiastical music can exist in modern times." The talent did exist, but in this instance the composer, though an Englishman, devoted it to the adornment of a ritual which cannot correctly be connected with English Church composers.

Wesley published very few things, for he had no confidence in the patronage of Church authorities. His fine Service in E was printed at the expense of his friend, Martin Cawood. His twelve anthems he caused to be printed and published by a literary firm in 1853, but he had as little belief in music publishers as he had in Cathedral clergy. He wrote few secular works besides glees, songs, and pianoforte pieces. His organ fugues were masterly, and written in keys which strangely contradicted his known views with regard to temperament.

Among his secular works may be named a fine cantata written for the opening of the Working Men's International Exhibition at the Agricultural Hall about the year 1869, and repeated several times since. He wrote three Services in the key of F, two of which were chant services, an evening Service in G, and a "Gloria" in C; all of which have been printed.

One of his most earnest hopes was to see Church music, and Church musicians, recognised according to their just dues. To enforce his views with respect to this matter, and to point out how that the composer, once a power in the state, the friend of kings, and the protected of monarchs, had become " a tradesman among musicans, and a musician among tradesmen;" he wrote the pamphlet alluded to, and addressed the Cathedral Commissioners to like effect. The brighter days he had longed to see never came with his life. His last words were, "Let me see the light." He sees it now.

Like his father, Wesley never believed himself to be treated with the respect due to his genius, but like his father also he continued to exercise the gifts he possessed, and to hope for recognition some time or another. This was accorded in the hearts of his countrymen and recognised outside. Spohr said, referring to his music, that it " is distinguished by a noble style, and by rich chosen harmonies as well as by surprisingly beautiful modulations;" and Dr. Walmisley of Cambridge, being asked his opinion of Wesley, said, "The universal consent of all musicians in England is that Dr. Wesley is the first among us, both for extraordinary talent, and for unwearied diligence in improving that talent to the utmost." For all this our musician " of extraordinary talent, and the first organ-player we have," ended his days as a country cathedral organist. He removed to Gloucester in 1865, and there he died on April 19th, 1876.

A reference to the last hours of Wesley, fitly introduces the name of one whose later years were spent in the darkness of blindness, but whose soul and spirits never lacked the inner light and cheerfulness.

It would be impossible here to give a long and exhaustive account of the life and labours of Henry Smart, although his name must be included amongst representative English Church composers, if only for the sake of his noble Service in F, which is well known and deservedly popular. A paraphrase of the twenty-third Psalm, "The Lord is my shepherd," is also a great favourite, and there are many of his anthems occasionally given, even if they are not so widely known as they might be. It is true that all these compositions are excellent, but, unlike his organ music and his secular writings, they do not represent any distinct rank in art, though they most worthily maintain a dignity of style. As a musician, the great honour he has earned is more for his power as a composer for the organ and for his charming songs and graceful part-songs, than for his anthems and pieces for the Church. In addition to those above mentioned he wrote a fine evening Service in G, and one in B flat, and a number of most beautiful hymn tunes in various collections, which entitle him to special distinction.

He also composed a sacred cantata entitled "Jacob," written for Glasgow in 1873, and many sacred songs and duets which belong properly to the region of domestic music. Much of his Organ music is frequently played in churches, and speaks of a mind of no common order.

Henry Smart was born in London in 1813, and died July 6th, 1879. The world at his death became conscious of the loss it had sustained, and began to do something to make amends for the inadequate encouragement it had given to his talent during his lifetime. He was named for a civil list pension, but did not live to enjoy it.

The want of proper encouragement was also experienced by the last musician on the present list of English Church composers. With the exception of one anthem, "Have mercy upon me," written for the Gresham prize in 1836, John Goss did not begin to write anthems until comparatively late in life; at all events, not until he was older than either Humfrey, Purcell, Wise, or Clarke, his predecessors, at the completion of their mortal career. This was simply from lack of interest shown towards his work. He had intended completing an anthem from each of the 150 Psalms, but never got beyond the first, "Blessed is the man," which was written in 1842, but which was not sung in St. Paul's, his own cathedral, until nearly twenty years after, when it was included in a collection of anthems made by Sir Frederick Ouseley. It is therefore not to be wondered at that he should have suffered his pen to remain idle. In 1852 he wrote the touching anthem, "If we believe," for the funeral of the Duke of Wellington, some time his patron, and in the year 1854, he wrote his sublime "Praise the Lord," for the bi-centenary Festival of the Sons of the Clergy. The whole of the musical world then became alive to the fact that there was a great genius in its midst, a genius whom circumstances had kept silent until he had arrived at the age when most men cease to speak. From that time forward, until within a few years of his death, he enriched the stores of Cathedral music with works "heard every day in one or other of our cathedrals, which preach the truths of religion more forcibly than many sermons."

John Goss was born on December 27th, 1800, at Fareham in Hampshire; his father, Joseph Goss, being organist of the parish church there. When just over eight years old he was sent to London to the care of his uncle Jeremiah, at that time a lay-vicar of Westminster Abbey, and deputy at St. Paul's and the Chapel Royal. Into the choir of this latter place he was admitted, and had for his master John Stafford Smith. At that time the education of the choristers was somewhat neglected. The boys taught each other the rudiments of music, the master marked and enforced progress by means of the cane, and reading and writing were taught by some one occasionally hired for that purpose by the master of the children. When young Goss left the choir, he became a pupil of Attwood for composition. His voice settled into a light and pleasing tenor very early, and to add to his allowance and make himself less a burden upon his relatives than he thought he was, he followed the usual custom at that time. He did not get an organ, so he accepted an offer to join the chorus at the opera, and in that capacity sang in the first representation of Mozart's *Don Giovanni* in this country in April, 1817. He continued his studies with Attwood, and learned to score for an orchestra with a facility equal to his inventive abilities. The fact of his being a singer made him mindful of the needs of vocalists, and nothing that he has ever written was not well laid out to display the best powers of the voice for which it is set. This is the secret of the success of his only opera, *The Soldier's Wife*, written about the year 1820, which enjoyed the unprecedented run, at that time, of over one hundred nights. This was also the reason of the immediate and lasting popularity of his *Six Glees and a Madrigal*, which he published in 1826. These include "Kitty Tell," "Ossian's Hymn to the Sun," "There is beauty on the mountain," "Hark! heard ye not?" and "The Sycamore Shade;" each or either of which have only to be heard to awaken the highest pleasure. In 1824 he was appointed by the Rev. J. Lockwood to the place of organist of the new church of St. Luke's, Chelsea, and here he remained for many years, doing his duty simply and honestly, and dividing his spare time between teaching and glee singing, for which his knowledge and taste made him much sought after. In 1827 he wrote an overture for the Philharmonic Society, which was highly spoken of. Neither his overture, nor any of the pieces in the opera "The Soldier's Wife," were ever published. "He had no desire," as he told a publisher who made him a very handsome offer for the latter, "that any one should lose money by publishing his works." In 1830 he printed, at his own risk, a collection of psalm and hymn tunes used at St. Luke's, Chelsea, and in 1833 his *Introduction to Harmony and Thorough Bass*, the first edition of which was fourteen years in selling, but fourteen more editions of which have subsequently appeared. This work was written for his pupils in the Royal Academy, with which institution he was connected for many years. When his master, "poor dear Attwood," died, in 1838, he was appointed organist of St. Paul's, chiefly though the interest of the Dukes of Cambridge and Wellington. With this appointment he was made a vicar-choral as usual. He greatly desired to institute some reforms in the service, which had become a very perfunctory matter, but his suggestions though kindly listened to were never acted upon. His active desires being thus crushed, he bcame a passive member of the Cathedral body, doing his duty in the most earnest and devotional manner. As an extempore player he exhibited great genius, and his introductory voluntaries to the anthems on Sunday afternoons have never been equalled, much less surpassed.

In 1854 he edited, in conjunction with the Rev. William Mercer, *The Church Psalter and Hymn Book*, and in 1856 he became composer to the Chapel Royal on the death of William Knyvett, and in the same year. He had some years before, in 1841, compiled a collection of chants. In his capacity as composer to the Chapel Royal as well as organist of St. Paul's he claimed the privilege of composing the music for the Thanksgiving Service for the recovery of the Prince of Wales in 1872. His modesty had kept him at first from asserting his right, and the long course of indifference with which he had been regarded had led him to refrain from taking any active steps in the matter, and but for the fact that his friends urged him to furnish the music for this state event as composer to the Chapel Royal, the greatest Church musician of his day would have been silent on a great national occasion when his voice ought to have been heard. Gounod, at that time a refugee in England, to show his gratitude to the country of his adoption, prepared a *Te Deum* for the same Festival, but it was not used. Goss contributed a fine anthem, " The Lord is my strength and my song," as well as the *Te Deum*, which is a masterpiece of musical construction, only marred in its completeness by the strange and, for him, very unusual treatment of the praises of " the Apostles, the Prophets, and the Martyrs." No one was ordinarily more careful in the use of the words of his sacred music than Goss was, or took more trouble to find the right and just expression to satisfy his own mind. He was almost fastidious in this respect. He might have felt under some disadvantage in the case alluded to, for the time each piece of music was expected to occupy was officially prescribed beforehand, and he may have fused the sentences to fit the time. As a rule he was as particular as to the accuracy of his text as he was in the endeavour to find the just musical expression and emphasis for it. It was well known to his intimate friends that he delayed the completion of his anthem, " O Saviour of the world," for some weeks, because he could not find the right chord to suit a certain passage in the words. Yet the whole seems so free and spontaneous that it is difficult to believe that it is not the result of a single uninterrupted effort. While the " Thanksgiving Service " was still in men's minds, the musical world was delighted to find that John Goss was to receive the well deserved honour of knighthood. Shortly afterwards he retired from active duty at St. Paul's, retaining his emoluments and the title of organist. Little by little he gradually relinquished active work, and a memorable mark of distinction at the close of a long and honourable career was reached when the University of Cambridge, in 1876, conferred upon him the degree of Doctor of Music, *honoris causâ.*

He died on May 10th, 1880, and was buried at Kensal Green cemetery; the first part of the funeral service being said in the Cathedral where he had been actual organist for thirty-four years, and nominal for forty-two. His name and fame had been spread abroad by means of his anthems, which are sung and loved wherever the English tongue is spoken. His music is always melodious and beautifully written for the voices, and is remarkable for a union of solidity and grace, with a certain unaffected native charm which will insure it a long life.

In the year 1867 his friends presented him with a noble service of plate; and in 1872 a subscription was collected, the proceeds of which were applied to the foundation in connection with the College of Organists of a Goss scholarship at the Royal Academy. The candidates for the scholarship were to be choristers who intend to devote themselves to the study of the organ.

With the name of John Goss the list of English Church composers of the past is concluded. The contributions of those that yet are living and striving to represent their views as to the treatment and character of Church music must stand for the future historian to deal with. He will be called upon to admire many efforts of genius and ingenuity, he will find much to praise and much to blame. He may possibly see how worthily the traditions of the school of Church music have been preserved throughout all the many political changes which have shaken and disturbed society; or he may find cause to lament the perversion of art by the concealment, or perhaps the destruction, of all those principles of taste and design which earned for the Church music of the past the respect and honour with which it has been regarded through a long series of years.

Further, the historian of the future may find that the many tricks of treatment which now seem to be adopted in obedience to some recognised but unwritten law, are struggles of truth with falsehood in a battle for the attainment of the once sacred fire, which inspired the souls of the Old English Church Composers. Out of all that now seems meretricious, new forms and ideas may arise which will induce posterity to give to the generation now passing by, a tribute of the highest praise for having initiated a movement which will be found to have tended to the expansion and development of Church music in its higher and nobler forms. The history of the past shows a constant if not a regular succession of graduated elevation and depression, more or less modified by outside impulses. If in the present day the candid historian is compelled to admit the existence of depressing influences, these may after all prove to be but the prelude to a corresponding elevation, and English Church Composers may again shine with a lustre equal to that which surrounded their progenitors at a time when the present becomes the past, and the future the present.

THE END.

LONDON: PRINTED BY BIA AND ITONBOULD, 224, BLACKFRIARS ROAD, S.E.

CPSIA information can be obtained
at www.ICGtesting.com
Printed in the USA
BVHW04*0913181018
530558BV00006B/23/P

9 780267 629213